FBI Tales

FBI Tales

By *Richard S. Clark*

Copyright © 2000 by Richard S. Clark

All rights reserved.
No part of this book may be reproduced, stored in a retrieval system, or transmitted by any means, electronic, mechanical, photocopying, recording, or otherwise, without written permission from the author.

ISBN: 1-58820-123-6

1stBooks – rev. 9/21/00

Table of Contents

Chapter Title

Not Another FBI Book 1
Training Wheels 3
Summer Camp in Siberia 5
Mittel Amerika 7
Toddling Town 9
Dress Code 11
Box of Candy 13
The Inspector 17
Foodnote-Cawfee 21
Bingo 23
Goodbye Chi 27
Indio Bonito 31
The Body 33
Fericking Around 37
Kidnaping With a Single "P" 39
The Indian from Indio 41
Blythe Spirits 45
The Great Train Escape 49
Me and Hoover Meet Again 51
The Rich Port 55
The Death of a Criminal Informant 57
Lookie Lookie Lookie 61
Shooting the Bull 63
El Aeropuerto 65
Whole Lotto Stuff Going On 67
Cuchi Cuchi Cuchillo 69

The Luminescent Limo	71
The Commissioner	73
Adiós Puerto Rico	75
Tampa Tales	77
Ybor City	79
One More for Ybor	81
Santos Trafficante	83
Top Ten Tunes	85
What! Time to Meet Hoover Again?	87
México Lindo	89
Dangereuse Foreign Liaison	91
The American Communist Group in Mexico (ACGM)	93
The Federales	97
The Jefatura	99
Feelthy Fotos	101
Mi Casa Es Su Casa	103
Pepe le Moco	105
The Judicial Police of the Federal District	109
Jesse James Roberts	111
Fuchi Mugre	115
The Mad Doctor	119
Comandante Peaches	121
Al Portador	123
The Grungy Genius	125
Post Script	131
Show Me Your Shard	133
Philip Agee	135
Sam the Man	137
Richard Scalzetti Cain	143
The True Cross	145
Body Surfing in Acapulco	147

Georgia on my Mind	151
Corazón de León	153
The Spy Who Came Down With A Cold	157
My Toughest Case	161
America Central	165
The A List	167
Miami Bound	171
Across the Agua to Managua	175
Ring Around the Rositas	177
Panama Cha Cha Cha	179
Where's My Transfer, Conductor?	181
Wrong Way to Tipperary	183
The Met – Scotland Yard	185
Vetting	189
Johnny and Clyde, Hoover and Homosexuality	191
The Troll on the Grassy Knoll	193

Not Another FBI Book

After some 30 moves in as many years we now live in La Jolla, California. La Jolla is a lovely place but infested with gaudy grey geezers. The greeting among these creatures is "What did you do?" meaning back when one was alive, real world. The response "FBI" provokes a reply incorporating "interesting", the dreaded description often applied to one's heirs and artwork. Well it was interesting, fascinating. If it was all that damn interesting there should be material for a book.

Wait, wait, come back. There are tales to be told, who killed JFK, was J. Edgar a sissy boy?

For some thirty years I was proudly and purposely a criminal case agent, meaning not one of them Washington weenies. A damned good agent, among the most decorated. It is the cases which should provide the interest, vignettes of actual cases, stitched together with a little personal embroidery.

The FBI was a very strange choice for a geeky, timid loner from Arizona. And vice versa. Absent father, hard-driving eccentric mother, shades of Lee Harvey Oswald. Billy Clinton for that matter. Whoa, got some grandiosity genes going here. The FBI was a dream since boyhood, leading me through three dreary years of law school. En route fortune favored me with a freckled gal from an even smaller flytrap, equally anxious to comb out the straw.

Shortly after law school whilst pursuing a career as a pop truck driver, a summons was received one fine Friday. Report to FBI HQ in DC Monday AM. Obviously a real recruit had fallen away. Not even time to clean the wedding and only suit. Mauve rayon, $18 off the rack.

No regrets. An engaging way to spend a life.

Training Wheels

To go from the rational, well-ordered world of law school to the weird wonderland of Hooverian HQ was a travel to another dimension. Everything seemed programmed to induce and maintain a state of terror. It was bad enough for the novitiates, already nervous as noodles in Nippon, but to see senior officials, by God G-men with decades of experience trembling from their wingtips to their fedoras was disconcerting. The theme seemed to be that of an omnipotent and malevolent supreme being eager to dispense ruthless punishment capriciously. Rather a lot like Lutheran catechism classes.

The very first day, the first hour, we were sworn in and given badges, which seemed to me like handing out chainsaws to children, particularly as I got to know my classmates. There was a dem and doser from Joisey who would have been arrested for overacting in a B gangster flic. He later became a sensational undercover agent and Agent in Charge.

There was a series of indoctrination lectures by some of the bizarre figures of the Hoover hierarchy, the main subject being the slavering idolatry of JEH, which seems like praising the Pope for piety.

A typical example was presented by Assistant Director Huge Kegg, a basso profundo known as "Troutmouth", because "Alligatormouth" doesn't have the same lilt. Kegg explained that the Great Man used to greet each new class personally but this was not possible with the many pressures. However, if anyone desired to meet Hoover it would be arranged. That is he had no time for us as a group but individually, hey no problem.

The second theme was the dire consequences of any infraction.

We were also issued a handbook, with the caveat that this was our bible, only more sensitive and valuable. This was a black loose-leaf about the size and sensitivity of the Phoenix phone book. The first few pages detailed transgressions, which would lead to dismissal with prejudice. This section grew daily to counter the daily evils committed by the field and soon overwhelmed the original manual. Any active agent automatically was in violation.

Another major theme was the dress code, critical for me because the merest glance revealed that I was fashion impaired. Genes. My father as a country croaker in Kansas sported about in a beret and riding boots, Dr. Kildare in Doug Fairbanks drag.

The code started with headgear. Hats mandatory. They checked the hat racks, hat police. Nobody wore hats but the Mafia and new agents. So at lunchtime we trotted off to the nearest haberdasher. Imagine, they had haberdashers. Most of us were lidless and clueless, easy marks. We came back looking like the Marx brothers. I got a Stetson, only brand I knew. Howdy podna.

Shortly thereafter I returned to my shabby rooming house and found to my horror that there was no handbook at hand for the required study. Rushing back to the greasy spoon I found it closed but there was my handbook on a shelf with my hat. Boy would the Russkies like to get their hands on them babies. Too bad the damned badge wasn't pinned to the hat.

The next step was clearly spelled out in the manual gleaming enticingly behind the greasy glass. Notify the Bureau immediately. They would send out a squad from the Washington Field office, awaken the Greek, retrieve the manual and drum me out of the corps with prejudice, the gutter guaranteed.

Or get some fitful sleep and pick it up in the morning with my grits and gravy, no one the wiser. An early lesson.

Summer Camp in Siberia

After weeks of studying the monumentally dull Rules and Regs we were bused off to Quantico. I always liked Quantico, a very handsome Marine base in the Virginia tidelands. It was like extended summer camp with demented counselors. Classes were day and night but not difficult, just tedious. Classwork was nothing compared to law school. The honor system was a joke. Lots of quizzes and passing was an obligatory 85. Typical Bureau. Hoover (and Hitler) set unrealistic standards and doomsday penalties, so there was a lot of fudging. Nobody failed, instructors would look bad.

The vaunted physical training was another joke, the chief instructor was a blimp. The Agent in Charge was looneytunes. Firearms were great fun. Marine Officer candidates were going through absolute hell by the numbers outside our front door and were incensed at our comparative coddling.

The food was great. They had an all black kitchen crew (and they claim Hoover was racist) who cooked up mountains of great fried chicken and gravy and mashed potatoes, greens, corn breads, puddings, this was five star stuff to a country boy.

Nobody had failed and graduation was just around the corner. And I was back in the soup. A ping pong ball was found in my bedtable. The recreation program, for which we were billed, consisted of a warped ping pong table in an adjoining bake oven barracks. Per regs I checked out a ball from the Chief Clerk. My bunkie, still a dear friend and the first of many micks to liven my life, wanted to play some more and said he would return the ball. Which he did, to my bedside, where it was found by the ping pong patrol.

I was summarily summoned to the august presence of the Special Agent in Charge. Rules were rules and balls were balls and if I had any I would have walked. I couldn't rat on my bastard bunkie, who later became a high bureau official in spite of his heedless hibernianism. So I did like any true son of the West. I groveled and survived with a stern warning.

We were all sick to death of this nonsense and desperate to learn our first office assignment. We had learned that all personnel decisions were dictated by vicious vindictiveness and feared for the worst. And I was very anxious to meet a young lady, born in my absence, who has graced our lives for an unbelievable 40 summers now.

Omaha, Nebraska. Doesn't carry the same cachet as say, Paris, France.

Mittel Amerika

After completing the four months of classwork our new family met in Omaha, Nebraska and started the adventure. Omaha was something of a training office and backwater but had a surprisingly rich criminal subculture. One of my classmates, who was a Navy carrier pilot and a real shaker and mover, was also assigned to Omaha. The son of a bitch went out and started solving crimes and developing informants and all that good stuff, right from the first day. Scared the snot out of the older agents, who we discovered were amazingly easy to frighten.

He was able and ambitious and should have zoomed to the top. In fact in his second office he became a full field supervisor, unthinkable. Then some buckos on his squad were caught bowling on bureau time and his career went into the tank. 20 years a street agent. That'll teach him.

After a spell in Omaha we bounced around Iowa a bit, nice people. The nicest was an older agent known as the Kindly Old Investigator. Most of us had yet to make an arrest and were anxious to witness some G-man action. Telephonic investigations were prohibited but the KOI would thumb through the directory and get on the line. "Is this the Jones house? Is Herbie home? Herbie, this is Joe Hughes down here at the FBI and we got a warrant for your arrest. Better get your butt down here. No, not right now, hell it's almost 5 o'clock. Get down here first thing in the morning."

And big ole Herb would be there at 9 sharp, hat in hand. Better looking hat than mine. His haberdasher was probably Harry Truman.

My work area covered a couple dozen counties but not much in the gangbusters department. Heartland, USA. Made my first arrest, solo, which was discouraged. Some homesick farm kid deserter, all of us nearly in tears. Never take me alive copper.

Closest I came to gunplay was a confrontation with a watch goose. No backing down this bastard, the big law meant nothing to him. His little head bobbing was a tough target and he knew it.

The first office apprenticeship was soon over. The next posting was Chicago, light years from Iowa. At least it wasn't New York whose legendary costs terrified us all. We were already broke and living in slums.

Toddling Town

Chicago was a poor place to apprentice in law enforcement, since local standards were so low. People pretty much presumed corruption. Cooperation with the law was bloody unlikely. Hoover had said there was no Mafia and one could see hoodlums on every corner with "MAFIA" embroidered on the brim of their Borsalinos. If they don't flaunt the colors how are the people to show respect? I think they got their dress code from the movies.

The police? I had police try to shake me down when I was driving one of the obvious black Ford G cars on official business. "Oh yeah, you know what a ticket costs in this town". (Cicero.) Buzz the badge in some bar and the bartender would whine Jeez we already paid you guys twice this week. No, No, sir, you don't understand, we are the federal law, not looking for gain but for your cooperation as a concerned citizen in locating a fugitive we believe to frequent your fine establishment. Sure.

Go into a station house where our fugitive had been booked in the past. Flash a mug foto from the San Francisco PD. Naw, heard of them Franciscos around Halsted but don't know any Sam.

Go into neighborhoods, perfectly decent, respectable neighborhoods, little girls skipping rope on the sidewalk. Little girls start chanting "L-A-V-A   L-A-V-A" (Sponsor's theme song on an FBI TV series) in time to their jumping. Shades come down, doors close. Nobody knew nuttin.

Three of us new agents hit Big Chi Town the same day and we all vowed we'd quit if we couldn't bust out within two years. The other two may still be there. The three of us got lucky and were assigned to the junior fugitive squad. It is hard to imagine anyone going into the FBI to do applicant work.

We found a ghastly slum basement flat on the West Side, enter from the alley dodging the flattened rats and ducking under the pipes and wires. Ottumwa looked pretty good. It took awhile to adjust to Chicago.

Dress Code

Mention has been made of the Bureau's fixation on attire. Hoover and his confidant Tolson regularly permitted themselves to be photographed cavorting in two-tone wingtips, pleated pants belted about the bustline and gabardine shirts. The inspectors enforcing the rules customarily wore snap brims and double-breasted sharkskins, zany zoot suits only a step from reet pleets.

A puzzle, especially for me since it is recognized that I am dyslexic in the dressing department. Poverty and poor taste are bad bedfellows. I wore denim from kinder through law school but I could never even get jeans right. In the land of Levis I got off brands with hammer loops and then turned the cuffs up like Cowboy Bob. When they got work holes, hell, I threw them away.

Upon reporting to Washington I had two suits. My wedding suit, a mauve rayon one button Sinatra model, $18 off the rack. And a Harris tweed. I loved that tweed. Bought it from a burned out vet for $10. Terrific guy, wounded in action several times, apparently while wearing the suit. But a little guy and the suit never fit.

It was a marvel anyway, never needed cleaning, just slurped up and digested dirt, gravy, whatever. It was scratchy and uncomfortable at any temperature above freezing. The weaver had heedlessly incorporated barbed wire, straw and sheep scat into the fabric. But absolute armor in the Windy City.

To complete this ensemble was an overcoat purchased for me by my mother. She had even worse taste than father, having pioneered muumuus and harlequin glasses on the plains. The overcoat was thick fleecy, flannelly wraparound, much like an indian blanket bathrobe.

This wardrobe didn't really make it in DC but some of the others looked just as silly. Summer was coming on and a swell Haspel cotton suit cost $25. Once in Quantico we wore the smart grey cotton "check your oil mister?" uniforms. Iowa and Nebraska were so far out in the sticks I could have worn bib overalls.

But Chicago was big city. And cold, lordy it was cold. Never mind, I had my Harris tweed with the cuffs a good foot above the slush, had my Stetson and ear muffs, had my bathrobe wrapped tight, galoshes with steel snaps. Looked like the Michelin man but I was ready. Bring on your worst, oh city with the broad shoulders.

I had my day-old peanut butter sandwiches in one overcoat pocket and my .38 Smith and Wesson Chief's Special in the other. Gotcha covered man.

Box of Candy

Aw, g'wan, you wanna ask if I ever shot anyone.

Naw, I never shot anyone, never involved in a gunfight. Rarely even had the gun out. In those days in Chicago there was a police lieutenant who had shot and killed something like a couple dozen delinquents. He was sort of a departmental designated hit man. And he was a public hero, medal and banquets and promotions. He shot one with a deer rifle. I wouldn't have been surprised if they strapped the body on the hood of a squad car for the Paddy's Day parade.

Naw, I never shot anyone. Came close once.

A lot of our fugitives were labeled "Armed and Dangerous", sort of a status thing. There were manual requirements but it didn't take much to earn an A&D merit badge. But this kid we knew was armed and had sworn never to be taken alive. His girl told us. Repeatedly.

Like a lot of our fugitives he was from an outlaw family. Not Mafia, just congenital outlaws. A lot of them were from the South, Southern Italy, South America, Dixie, South Poland. The strong sun breaks down the fiber of narrow Northern knothole nicety.

They let you know right away, that blank look. FBI, we're looking for Tony. Tony, Tony, I don known any Tony. Your son Tony. Oh that Tony, he don come around any more. He was here yesterday. Tony? Yesterday? Sez who? His mother. His mother? She's crazy everybody knows that.

My partner and I had been looking for this Tony for a long time. His family had a junkyard a couple of miles deep in the Chicago River swamps.

The place was virtually unassailable. Any approach alerted the proverbial dogs and forget about searching a junkyard.

Tony had illusions of gangsterhood and a little moll he used to knock up and knock down. After a beating she came around to snitch on him. She is the one who told us he always had a gun in his waistband and swore never to be taken alive. Have a nice day.

One day he was going to rendezvous with this dolly at an intersection on the South side. We knew his car, a terrible old clunker, like a Terraplane. And we knew the hour. So we signed out a G car and staked out the corner.

Auto lotto was a big game in the old Bureau, especially in the big cities. Cars were not assigned and there was a wide discrepancy in quality, from a Cadillac strictly reserved for Hoover's rare visits to a Studebaker wagon. Covered wagon.

The premier ponies were the 1951 Ford Interceptors but we junior G-men rarely got a hot item like the Interceptor. They were reserved for the cigar squad (major cases) to race down to Indiana for non-union haircuts.

But this time we got an Interceptor and parked at the corner and waited. And waited. And waited. A few sparkling crystals of snow wafted waywardly down for a momentary display on the tawdry tram tracks. Then it began to snow like a son of a bitch. The Interceptor was actually a big pain in the butt in Chicago because idling was not in its vocabulary. It was difficult to keep the car warm and the windshield clear.

Finally, the Terraplane lumbered up and the jill jumped in.

We engaged our glands and gears in pursuit mode and proceeded to slither madly all over the tracks. The Interceptor simply wouldn't throttle down enough to maintain traction and fulfill its nom de guerre. The old roadster made a clean getaway at a stately 6 mph. Probably never heard the siren. Thought the red lights were Christmas.

This guy was beginning to make us look bad.

The next phase found me sitting on the same damned coupe but with a better screenplay. We learned that the subject was accustomed to stashing the car in the neighborhoods along the riverbank. When trouble loomed he would gandydance over the railroad bridge and drive away. We found the Terraplane parked in front of one of those typical Chicago neighborhood taverns which so enjoyed visits from the law. I camped in the flyspeckled front window of the tavern. My buddy parked a block away and by radio arranged for a car to drive up the river road. Regular undercover car, black Ford four door with spotlights and antennae like a monster praying mantis.

The regulars in the bar didn't seem to be concerned by the sight of a sweaty young stranger in a Stetson and bathrobe eyeballing the bleak boulevard. This was Chicago, these were sophisticates.

Worked a treat. Soon enough our friend was traipsing across the ties and leaping into his car. I came boiling out of the bar and shoved my Chief's Special in his ear shrilly screaming "FBI HANDS UP" in my manly falsetto.

He was pretty cool, he'd seen this movie a dozen times. He didn't move and he would not put his hands up. He kept insisting he had to get something out of his belt, exactly where the girl claimed he kept his gun.

I thought OH CHRIST gonna have to shoot this bastard, be filling forms for a year. But I figured I had time to at least see the gun before I shot him. Meanwhile I am screaming and waving my off arm like a mad windmill. The folks in the tavern were entranced by all this action on the really big screen.

Finally my colleague rolled up and we get the guy out and braced and cuffed. Naturally checked the waistband first thing, no gun, just a small box. Box of candy.

Candy for the girl who got him captured and damn near got him killed. Maybe wanted him killed.

The Inspector

In spite of involvement with police all over the country and all over the world the meaning of "Inspector" remains unclear to me. Some departments have all Inspectors, some have none. Within the Bureau there was no mystery. Inspectors actually inspected and reported directly to the deity. Even Agents in Charge trembled in their presence. Somebody always got hurt when an Inspector passed through.

Everyone on fugitive work had been turned out to look for a badly wanted fugitive. He was badly wanted because of a report that he claimed to have access to the sacred FBI files. Through an FBI employee. Very big stuff indeed. So big that a full bore Inspector was even then on his way out from Washington to coordinate the matter. We were up to our earflaps in cow flop if we didn't catch this guy.

Several of us had interviewed his girl friend that afternoon with no great success. But later that evening there was a report that the fugitive was to arrive at O'Hare Airport about 9 PM. They called me because I lived closest to the airport and could identify the girl, who was expected to meet him. I tooled out alone in my faithful Chevvie. There was no time to check out a G car or get a backup, which was usually the case. We weren't supposed to do arrests solo and weren't given mileage but the back seat of the Chevvie was befouled by many a filthy fugitive in the next couple of years.

I raced out to O'Hare to check the waiting room. Neither the flight nor the airlines were known. Whoa, this wasn't Omaha, there were a dozen airlines, a dozen waiting rooms, strung out on a long corridor. The root of "corridor" means to run. I ran, frantically, back and forth, one end to the other, a fleeting figure with a bathrobe flapping and flying behind. Never did see the girl.

Maybe she saw me first, the same weird kid wearing a Stetson who interviewed her earlier, a miscast McCloud.

Some backup help arrived but no joy resulted. We spent the rest of the night camped on her house and finally caught up with the guy the next afternoon.

Our instructions were to leave the interrogation strictly to the Inspector. This was far too sensitive a matter to leave to field hands. So we hardly said a word to the guy, took him straight to the FBI office. That was fine with us, we couldn't wait to see a legendary bull Inspector in action, wondering what tack the demon investigator would choose.

The Inspector came roaring into the interview room and grabbed the guy and started screaming at him. "What the ----- is all this ---- about you getting ---- from FBI files!" was how he started and it went downhill thereafter. Now this technique probably worked great when used on sniveling helpless FBI agents, his usual victims, but the finesse was lost on this kid who had been screamed and sworn at all his life. His mom probably carried on worse when he kiped cookies.

He wouldn't admit anything. Which was ironic because the rest of us in the room realized that the kid could have confessed to anything, anything at all, including the substantive crime for which he was fugitive, and walked. Free as a bird.

First of all this type of abuse was foolish, counter-productive and probably illegal. And second no one had laid a Miranda warning on the kid, required even then in federal court. Heaven knows what the Inspector expected. Did he expect we would perjure ourselves on these fine points? He was a wonderful example of Bureau expertise and was soon on his way back to neverneverland.

There was a probably apocryphal story that once Troutmouth Kegg trained out to Chicago as an Inspector in response to a letter obviously from a Chicago agent, detailing the many flaws of Mr. Hoover and the Bureau, and signing himself "The Shadow". Kegg got up in front of the whole office and demanded that the Shadow be man enough to come forth and claim responsibility. He waited vainly in his office until long past the deadline and finally broodingly boarded the train back to D.C.

And on the train he was handed a telegram. "Come back, I am ready to confess. The Shadow". Kegg was an educator by profession. Has anyone ever seen this ploy work in the schools?

Foodnote-Cawfee

Among the many idiot policies that characterized Hooverlandia was an absolute injunction against coffee breaks. This for grown men who were working terrible hours out in all kinds of weather. And a lot of this work was done with and through cops who pretty much live on coffee and were only too aware of this ridiculous rule. Like all the Hoovermania there were no exceptions, no appeal and severe penalties. Censure, suspension, and most dreaded, transfer.

So there was the degrading spectacle of Agents in Charge and Inspectors trying to make their bones by busting agents in the local coffee shops and literally destroying careers and lives. It was impossible to work around the clock without some intake so as well be hung for a lion as a lamb.

Like most of the Draconian decrees it was largely ignored. Neither Hoover nor Mussolini ever learned this simple lesson.

Cementhead Muldoon was one of the Agents in Charge in Chicago and later became an Assistant Director, one of the apostles. He would personally track down and discipline coffee drinkers. None of that crap on my watch, mister. The Mafia was running away with our major cities and Hoover was promoting Cementhead for breaking java junkies.

One day one of the older guys, a relief supervisor, very untypically and surreptitiously motioned me to join him as we left the office. He was one of those shufflers whose spirit had been broken. The Bureau abounded in these sad types. I didn't think romance was involved although a favored prank of the old guard was to wink and blow secret kisses at the new lads.

What now. I dutifully followed this creepo down a tortured trail through underground Chicago. If you knew the ropes and routes you could move all over the loop below ground. This was enormously helpful in inclement weather, which was the only brand available locally. We ended up at Sears' basement cafeteria. Two supposedly grown G-men skulking a mile through the sewers for a mug of bad coffee. He thought he was doing me a big favor, this is how the big law operates in the big city. Jesus, Joseph and Mary where do I go to confess. Man I don't even like coffee, much less bad company.

If coffee destroyed careers what in the world was the penalty for drinking. Yet there were plenty of pretty flagrant alkies in every office. Another test and treat for the new guys was invitation to lunch at the Berghoff, a wonderful old-style stand-up tavern in the heart of the loop. They had absolutely fabulous corned beef sandwiches, which begged for the company of beer. Drink orders were deferred until the new guy made his choice, not aided by the famously surly help. Are you with us or against us?

It was a tough choice. The dark was delicious but the light seemed to go better with the sharp mustard.

Bingo

Building a solid case for criminal prosecution, identifying the perpetrators and gathering the necessary evidence can be pretty tedious. But once arrest process is issued, locating and arresting the fugitive is quite enjoyable, even for a sissy like your servant. Thanks to the Unlawful Flight statutes a lot of the FBI work was fugitive work and it was engrossing, like a really big game hunt, a mental exercise and adrenal rush.

My regular partner was the son of a mick cop from the East, like a lot of the agents of that era. The EX SA's directory looks like the Dublin phone book. We began to build a rep as a team, sometimes scoring 2 or 3 apprehensions in a day. They even asked us to the exclusive major case squad.

I loved fugitive work but I hated searching houses. You were on the subject's home turf, the outlaw's family and neighbors were firmly united against the law, those old rattrap tenements were full of hiding places, you couldn't close all the exits, and it just wasn't seemly to go around waving a pistol.

Once we got a call that a fugitive was in a certain flat on the south side. When we got there the flat was full of hostile blacks. That was not usual in those days, the hostility. Only later was it even a requirement to work double in those areas. But we had only a vague description of the subject, how were we going to sort through all these people? My partner was gassing with them and I started nosing around the place. No permission was necessary since no one would acknowledge any proprietary interest in the premises. I was poking around in a dark closet when a voice issued from the depths "Don't shoot, put down the gun, I'm your man".

Gun? What gun? I looked down and damned if there wasn't a pistol in my hand. And I hadn't even consciously been aware there was someone in the closet. Lightnin' Jack. Maybe there was something to the training after all.

Another time I was searching a house and found the subject under his bed. Under his bed, like I was the closet monster. Probably had his banky. And he wouldn't come out. I yelled and screamed and he wouldn't budge. Maybe he thought I would just go away. Finally I grabbed a leg and just ripped him out of his sanctuary. Unfortunately the bed had those old steel springs and it raked him like a harrow. He looked like a goldbrick on the Bounty. I felt awful. This was going to ruin the back seat.

We had another fugitive from an outlaw family in the scrap business. They had a big house on the west side and it was stuffed with junk, floor to ceiling, wall to wall, roof to basement. The supervisor asked if we searched the place. Supervisors don't understand stuff. Sure we did, chief. Shit the family gleefully invited us to do our best. There were undoubtedly crawlways through this crap but it would take months. How I envy modern uniforms with their dogs for this work.

They were beginning to make us look bad. I looked pretty bad anyway but Jim had a natty surplus trench coat with grenade loops. At least I had ditched the Stetson. I got a homburg and he got a bowler at a sidewalk sale. Two bits each. Seriously. To be busted by these two was a physical and style humiliation.

We would periodically stake out the residence and neighborhood and knew some of their cars. Actually they raced junkers. Finally BINGO, spotted him at the wheel of a huge black Lincoln parked a block from his home.

I pulled in front to cut him off and Jim jumped out to collar him. He had other ideas. His motor was running and he jumped the clutch and the curb and it was off to the races.

Code three, siren wailing its sinister song, red lights bringing a momentary glow to the pale cheeks of the bums lining West Madison. These chase scenes were not all that frequent in the FBI and unfortunately we didn't have an Interceptor that day of all days. The pursuit went on for miles.

A Chicago cop had been killed that week and that pretty much pumped up the pulse of the usually lethargic local law. Soon we had picked up a trailing train of black and whites who counterpointed the siren symphony. We had no radio communication with them, they were chasing two black Ford sedans maniacally maneuvering through heavy traffic, I could see assorted firearms waving out windows. When I finally boxed the kid in there were a dozen guns pointed at us as the cop cars growled up. I was petrified. Of my fellow officers. Getting too old for this business, burned out at 24.

Goodbye Chi

Chicago was a horrible place to be assigned in those days. It had all the evils of New York without the panache. It was expensive. The climate was dreadful. Spring and fall could be nice if they sprang and fell on weekends. The rest of the time it was colder than a Klondike Quickfreeze or hotter than Satan's sauna. We had another golden-haired girl who didn't sleep the first year of her life and therefore felt that none should slumber. It took an hour to weatherproof the GHGs for a walk in the park where the zanies would fondle them.

Through influential relatives we fell into a rent frozen apartment near Lincoln Park which we furnished from Railroad Salvage. Fine place but not safe. Our nice neighborhood grocer had himself personally shot to death 3 or 4 robbers. He would submit and then plug them as they went out the door. Have a nice day.

And there were bears in the basement. Well, not really, but that is what I told the GHG to keep them away from the furnace and they spent the rest of their infancy huddled in the hall closet.

Busting out of Chicago was the main topic in the squadroom, very like prison. The Bureau had a job staffing the big cities. Scuttlebutt had it that the only way out was a disciplinary transfer, a common and costly punishment.

We had one very senior agent on the fugitive squad, a wonderful, salty, example for us apprentice agents, sharp contrast to the many craven, truckling toadies. First class professional agent. It was a pleasure and an honor to work with him. Any simple arrest was a work of art.

But he was unlucky. He was on his third disciplinary transfer. And he had done nothing wrong. Once some idiot agent wrote Hoover a long letter about all that was wrong with the Bureau and included George's name as among those who agreed. Another time during an interrogation the subject grabbed his partner's pistol and shot himself. George said he didn't mind the suspensions and censures but the transfers were killing him. He was by far the best agent on the squad.

But the threat of a disciplinary transfer out of Chicago was hollow. Butte and Anchorage were the standard disciplinary destinations and guys were lined up to go. An oft considered ploy was dropping a handbook in the Chicago River but it was felt that one would have to include the pistol and badge to get the job done.

One loophole was the language program. This was dangerous because one could spend the remaining years in some cubbyhole with a headset compressing your brain listening to loud, incomprehensible Balkan gibberish about imaginary sexual exploits. Rock and Roll in other words.

But Spanish. That was intriguing. I loved the sound and the potential. Most of the offices needing Spanish speakers were under the rustle of the royal palm.

Nearly anyone from Arizona spoke a little rudimentary Spanish. I got a cheat sheet and passed the Spanish exam and was detailed to Spanish School. There were two Spanish schools, one on an easygoing Army base on the beautiful Monterrey Peninsula. The other in the sweatbox of the Identification Division in D.C. Whatever, we were out of Chicago.

Actually it wasn't bad duty. The old Ident building was far removed from FBI HQ and stuffed with Midwest nubility. The Bureau combed the plains to dragoon farmer's daughters for the mind-numbing fingerprint and filing work. There was a huge turnover and a scandal a week. Some of the help were humping on Hoover's time.

We got a nice little flat in the Southeast and actually made some friends, lived like real life people. The classwork was dull but as always everyone was above average. We all passed even though we couldn't actually speak Spanish except to each other. And it was time again for the Bureau to play lottery with our lives.

Attendance at Spanish school was predicated on assignment to Spanish speaking offices and eventual assignment to San Juan, Puerto Rico. San Juan was difficult to staff, few wanted to go there and the logical solution, recruitment of locals, was unthinkable. The locals tended to the darker hues. The Spanish deficient offices were the baleful New York and those highly desirable offices shaded by the palm.

To our delight we were assigned to San Diego, our number one office of preference. The Master lies in wait for those she finds presumptuous. This paradise had two purgatories, two RA's (Resident Agencies, not red arses) known and dreaded throughout the Bureau. El Centro, along the Mexican border, and the even worse one-man post located below sea level in Indio. Everyone in Arizona knew Indio. That was where one gassed up and rinsed off the vomit enroute to the fabled beaches of CALIFORNIA.

I checked into the San Diego office at 8 AM and by 10 AM we were tooling over the mountains to Indio, tears torrenting down the freckled cheeks of the child bride from Chandler.

Indio Bonito

Indio was considered the craphole of California but it wasn't a bad assignment. The weather was wonderful in the winter. Palm Springs was right next door and the desert was littered with LA Glitterati. I loved being a one-man Resident Agent (RA), Lone Wolf Gonzalez. Hoover hated RAs, because they were that much further away from supervision. Most HQ agents dreaded assignment to the RAs, rusticated and removed from the bright lights.

The larger RAs, like Riverside and Des Moines, were just little field offices. The smaller 3 and 3 man offices were notorious breeding grounds for bad feelings. A common situation was a two man RA where neither had spoken in years, a marriage gone bad. A one man RA was just right, a great place to learn my trade, with the help of the local law and the super senior agents in Riverside. If the phone rang or the teletype chattered, as they did daily, there was only little me at the end of the line.

The cops were great. They were used to operating on their own in remote areas with scant resources. They ragged me a lot but were glad to have me around. There was a fantastic degree of cooperation among the many agencies, police, sheriffs, highway and border patrols.

There was a lot of travel. My territory was bigger than Vermont and maybe more active. Every month I had to report to headquarters for conferences, file reviews, firearms, federal court, whatever, generally a 12-hour day.

The freckled DG stopped weeping after a bit. She was pretty busy with two more kids in two years. What was causing this? They are grown now and still bitter about having to list this as their birthplace. We bought a little stucco ranch for $12,000, try that in Chicago. Friends and family from Arizona could visit easily. And quickly. Few cared to linger long in Indio. We made some friends, some still friends, nice folks in small towns. We are living almost like real life people.

Summers were terrible but no worse than Arizona. Never dipped below 100 day or night June through September. Once in awhile the Lord would remember us and send an actual plague of locusts.

Every year our lives were brightened by the Riverside County Fair and Date Festival. The local specialty is the date shake. The aroma of regurgitated date shake frying on the sizzling sidewalk was the essence of Indio. That and the local kids tarted up like Aladdin dancing across the stage dodging camel ca ca.

But we knew we were in a fool's paradise. Puerto Rico loomed ominously and unavoidably.

The Body

Her inexpressibly perfect face rested against my shoulder. My arms protectively enclosed her fragile delicacy. She was the loveliest creature imaginable, exquisite features, porcelain skin, luminescent eyes, crowning a world famous figure. She was a MOVIE STAR. Gorgeous, glamorous and glimmering. She was in terrible trouble and looking to me for help. Headlines around the world shrieked of her disappearance and here she was, supposedly safe in my arms. All Hell was about to bust loose. Sure wisht I'd had a camera.

Marie MacDonald was a second tier sex kitten known as "The Body", a faux Monroe. She had vanished mysteriously and there was enormous media interest. Now here she was folded in my arms in a tiny, tinny hospital in Indio, California. It was well after midnight. A truck driver, proverbial knight of the plight, found her on a bridge in the bleak desert highlands and brought her to Indio. I was summoned because it was presumed to be a kidnapping and I was the federal law. Twenty-five years old and the only FBI for 100 miles.

Indio wasn't the fundament of the world. That was in Thermal, a hair to the south and closer to Hell. Indio was where good Zonies hope their cars don't break down on their way to the beach. "Zonie" is what Californians call people from Arizona, with the same ambivalent affection Mexicans give to "Gringo". We were Zonies. What were we doing in this even drearier desert.

Marie was pretty darn cuddly but not particularly coherent, possibly her usual state. A cursory exam by the kindly croaker at the claptrap clinic found nothing seriously amiss and she had been given a sedative. She rambled on about having been abducted and held in the desert by a dark man. She was affirmative but uncommunicative on the sexual assault issue, also perhaps the usual. She was packed off to bed but there was mighty little rest for many in the Coachella Valley the next few days.

I called my chief in Los Angeles, who had also been my jefe in Chicago. Cementhead Muldoon. Muldoon was a famous Bureau character who combined Murphy's law with the Peter Principle. He loved to roar around town in his custom Ford Interceptor with sirens blaring to interfere with otherwise sedate apprehensions. And he loved to mix with the movie mob.

There was no indication of interstate transportation and therefore no apparent federal jurisdiction. In fact the matter of jurisdiction was never resolved. For that matter it was never resolved whether there had actually been a crime.

The whole scenario was all too reminiscent of the tale of the evangelist Aimee Semple MacPherson, who had disappeared into the desert decades earlier with a tambourine man.

There was only one phone in this small sanatorium and it started bouncing around the desk demanding attention. The caller identified himself haughtily as Reuters. From London. England. Ronald Effing Coleman. This was within two hours of her rescue. It was just the beginning.

By dawn the next day media from around the world began converging on the little Sheriff's Substation. The Sheriff had assumed jurisdiction in the absence of any positive position by your humble servant. A TV crew came galloping up demanding to know the location where she had been found. "The bridge over Weaver Wash". "Where's that?" "About 27 miles East." "Too far, where's the nearest bridge?" they demanded, tearing off to fulfill the heavy obligation of informing the public.

A specialist OB-GYN was called in from the big city, Riverside, for a more detailed examination. It appeared that confirmation of sexual assault was not conclusive in this experienced woman. However by golly he did find a huge, hitherto unmentioned, diamond ring in the far reaches of her undoubtedly decorative declivity. He apparently had a longer reach than the local talent.

This was considered highly significant, to be treated with the utmost confidentiality. As far as I knew only the Obie, the Sheriff and I were privy to this information, which was duly relayed to Cementhead.

When I finally got home after working around the clock for a couple of days, I popped a beer and turned on the TV. At that time there was a very popular, funny, lippy TV personality in LA named Tom Duggan. Come to think of it he was also a Celt from Chicago.

Duggan was reporting in his characteristic caustic way about the Marie MacDonald caper. He said there were reports that a diamond ring had been found on her person. "That's hitting below the belt" was how he phrased it.

Desi Arnaz and Lucille Ball, megastars at that time, lived nearby in Palm Springs and were friends of Marie, good friends indeed. They were extremely supportive and checked on her constantly. They would contact me for updates, giving me mini-celebrity status. On checking for messages at the station the staff would whoop "Oh Deek, chew suppose to call Desi" and fall on the floor.

The matter was never satisfactorily resolved. Desi stopped calling. A grand jury considered whether to charge her with filing a false crime report but no true bill was returned, perhaps because the fine Renfrew-of-the-Mounties Sergeant assigned to the case tended to believe her.

I had my doubts. She certainly didn't look like she had been kidnapped and assaulted and left in the desert. She looked like she was auditioning for "Girl of the Golden West." I sure wish I had a foto. And maybe an autograph. Maybe on a signed statement.

Fericking Around

Being the lone federal law involved getting involved in a lot of exciting cases. One of my first cases was a lead to check a print shop in Indio where a fugitive was formerly employed. The lead was by airtel, a typical Bureau invention, supposedly with the same priority as a teletype but sent by airmail to cut costs. That means the information arrived as slowly as regular correspondence but with less detail. But it was on blue paper, just like the real thing.

Such leads were rarely productive and I must admit I didn't even review this sparse data before checking at the print shop. "Charlie? You looking for Charlie? Hey Charlie, this federal man over here is looking for you." This shook me up a bit but Charlie ambled over amiably and agreeably submitted to arrest.

But understandably Charlie wanted to know why he was arrested. That sounded like a reasonable request but I had not the vaguest idea. The airtel was headed with his name and the charge, in teletype shorthand. In this case FERIC. The FBI had jurisdiction over a couple of hundred sundry crimes but I had never heard of FERIC and didn't suppose he had either.

The airtel contained a description, and he agreed he was this particular Charlie. And the details of the warrant, charging violation of Title 18, Section 3570, Untied States Code. So I leveled with him and informed him that he was under arrest for violation of Title 18, Section 3570 U.S. Code.

It reminded me of my favorite scene from my favorite movie "Gunga Din" when Cary Grant marched into the lair of a thousand murderous thugees to announce in his inimitable (but all too frequently imitated) way "You are all under arrest, and you know what for too."

Charlie felt he was entitled to a little more and I was curious myself. So I drove us across the tracks to my office, our back bedroom, to check the manuals. FERIC stood for False Entries in the Records of an Interstate Carrier. That's what for, you animal.

Little the wiser we chased the sun across the desert to Riverside for appearance before the U.S. Commissioner. He was more than agreeable to a release on recognizance and we were all in our home beds that night.

It turned out Charlie had been a station agent with the Southern Pacific and got careless with the ticket proceeds. Regular Dillinger.

A few days later the owner of the print shop called. Charlie had gotten himself arrested again by some supposed federal agents. Took several calls to find out some eager marshals from LA had seen this warrant and figured it was a good chance for some mileage and a day in the desert. Two of them. Probably an air-conditioned car.

Charlie was already finished with the Southern Pacific and now his printing future was dodgy.

Serves him right. Out West we don't cotton to that FERIC stuff, right Chester?

Kidnaping With a Single "P"

Years later I found myself at the podium of a huge auditorium at Scotland Yard in London stuffed with police executives from all over the world. I was supposed to address them on the subject of kidnaping, a field in which the FBI was justly considered pre-eminent. As usual I had prepared by sinking into a depressed coma and searching my soul in vain for any sign of expertise in this field.

But actually over the years I had worked on hundreds of kidnap cases, we all had. And we all hated these cases. They are very difficult to resolve and Hoover put enormous pressure on these cases. Above all there is the consideration for the innocent victim, whose life may be forfeited for any mistake.

The Greenlease Kidnaping was the hottest case in the Bureau. The victim was the infant son of a prominent Midwest family. Kidnaping was top priority and I regret to reveal that more prominent folks got more priority. Like all such cases the more pressure and publicity, the more leads are generated. Probably 98% of the effort goes into running down false leads, all of which must be treated as genuine.

I got a call relaying an anonymous report that there was a mysterious lady living in a shack in Palm Springs with a baby that might be the Greenlease victim. Not an impossible scenario.

I shot over to Palm Springs and checked the neighborhood. Sure enough the neighbors all knew this suspicious, surly, secretive lady who lived in the shack, zealously and jealously guarding a male infant with the general characteristics of the Greenlease victim. She had moved there about the time of the kidnaping and seemed clearly to be hiding out under a false identity.

What to do. Textbook would be to set up a round the clock surveillance possibly with electronic assistance until the lady and the child could be identified. At least a dozen people full time for a week or more…well beyond anything I was likely to get.

Uncharacteristically I took the bull by the horns and banged on the sagging screen door. The lady was as advertised. One of those aggressive big city broads with an attitude and a half. Hates cops or any authority. Don know nuttin, ain't gonna say nuttin, no documents or explanation for the kid, none of my goddam business, not about to let me in, 120 in the meager shade of a mangy mesquite.

Gonna be hard to resolve this one to Mr. Hoover's satisfaction. And it has to be resolved. Then. Because if it is the victim they are good as gone. Shoulda been a shoe salesman.

But she is holding the naked, squalling baby.

The Greenlease victim was circumcised. A razor's edge resolution.

The Indian from Indio

When I was a kid I resolved never to get into the medical dodge because our lives were forever being disrupted by the late night phone calls. Now our kids feel the same about the FBI. Only decades later did I learn that a lot of dad's calls were from dollies.

Another late, urgent call. Even as we spoke a badly wanted fugitive was making a call from the pay phone in the bus depot of Indio. The depot was a favored hangout for the local bon vivants because it was open late not picky. The reek of rancid grease and diesel fumes provided overtones to the sour stench of puke and piss.

The fugitive was wanted for a series of rough store stickups all over the Midwest. Known to be heavily armed, extremely dangerous, approach with caution, all that good stuff, me the only fed for 100 miles around. But I called the Indio PD and glory be to God Homer was there, as he usually was.

Homer was the Chief of Detectives and also the only detective on the tiny force. He was a little guy with a bad eye but plenty capable and I was damn glad he was around.

We met at the PD and decided to go to the depot in the old non-descript G car. There were two big young uniform bucks on duty, eager to be part of the show, but the last thing we needed was a black and white on the scene, so they were on standby. It wasn't going to be a walk in the park. We only had a description and the place was jammed with the same sort of Southwest low life we were looking for.

Just as we pulled up across the depot an enormous, feloniously drunk Indian came staggering out and lurched around his pickup searching doggedly for the door. Homer knew him and so did I.

The Coachella Valley was sprinkled with a number of small, sad, scruffy Indian Reservations. The tribes had rights to plots with potential value. Sharkskins from LA were forever Buicking out to the desert to exchange beads for leases. Crime on the Reservation was federal and I had tried several times to interview this guy, but he was always too drunk. Finally I went to the reservation practically daybreak and found him only semi-comatose and got a statement. Only he wouldn't talk to any damned G-man who wouldn't drink with him. Dago red straight from the jug and warm as pony piddle at 8 AM on a hot desert day. Refreshingly tangy actually.

The tribe was small but the braves were huge, Samoan size, and notoriously difficult to handle when drunk, pretty much all the time. They were legendary among local lawmen and I think every male in this family came to a violent end. Homer had built a certain rep and rapport and had arrested this guy several times by himself. Like a lot of old cops he knew bullshit was better than a billy.

Homer just couldn't let this guy drive away. He had already drawn a crowd and was cosmically crocked and would have killed somebody. So he went over to chat with his chum and they were getting along gangbusters.

Homer gave me a wink with the good eye, which I took to mean everything was Jake, call up the backup and get this guy off scene so we could get on with our business.

The patrolmen rolled up with their glands in gear and grabbed hold of Sequoia. Big mistake. Little Bighorn. Next thing I know they are flying through the air like a huge centrifuge. My fault so figured I'd better hump in. I waited for a clear shot at his billboard-size back and leapt in and levered him to the ground with a bar armlock. Holy Shit it worked! Hurrah training school.

I got some cuffs on him and was working him into the squad car and the officers said to leave it to them. Another big mistake.

I joined Homer and the loafers on the curb for the rest of the riot. This crowd was basically Indian fans and cheered whenever their hero scored a goal. Finally they overwhelmed him and drove off to the station.

We turned our attention to the depot but it was abandoned. Everyone had decided the neighborhood was deteriorating and decamped. Another long night wasted futilely checking local flops. Our guy was long gone. Big Chief was released, no charges, no hard feelings.

Indio is a Spanish word. Means Indian. In Mexico one often hears it used as a pejorative. Mexicans are forever accusing gringos of being racist.

Blythe Spirits

Blythe, California is surely the most inappropriately named place on the planet. It perches on the banks of the opaque Colorado River, which demarks the lunar landscapes of Arizona from the desolate deserts of California. Zonies hated it worse even than Indio, a pit stop in purgatory, with the beaches still far over the horizon.

There were agricultural inspection stations on both sides where one queued up to lie about contraband fruit. Naturally the clientele was choking mad with thirst and raced to the water cooler, to the delight of the Inspectors, who otherwise had a boring job in a bakehole. The visitor would gulp and then gasp. Blythe water was terrible, better off to pee in your water bag. You can imagine the coffee.

Blythe was the eastern terminus of my territory and called for a couple of days a month. The funny thing was I had worked in Blythe before. After VJ day jobs became scarce and some labor contractor signed up a bunch of us to work on the railroad docks in Blythe icing produce cars. Horrible job, minimum wage, manhandling 300-pound ice blocks, living in a labor camp on cold canned beans and crapping in a crab-ridden outhouse. A block fell and crushed my foot and I was the happiest crip in Southern California.

Blythe wasn't totally terrible. There was a golf club. They used pickups as golf carts. Seriously. And there were far worse places in the territory. Remember "Bad Day at Black Rock"? Black Rock was about 20 miles west of Blythe. Halfway between Blythe and Indio was Desert Center, the fiefdom of Desert Steve Ragsdale. Desert Steve made Gabby Hayes look like Fred Astaire. The bunkhouse-motel there was a famous tarantula habitat.

South of Blythe, along the river, was no man's land. The river constantly changed course leaving a lot of loops where jurisdiction was a joke. These areas were popular with outlaws and there were places the local law, who were plenty tough, wouldn't go after dark.

I didn't much enjoy traveling to Blythe and I hated making an arrest there. Any fugitive arrested had to be transported by your servant 175 miles across the desert to the U.S. Commissioner and federal-approved lockup in Riverside. As the most junior agent with the biggest territory I was awarded the worst car. A journey this long meant we had to eat and widdle and at least one of us was broke and wearing handcuffs. So basically I tried not to arrest anyone in Blythe much after noon.

Sometimes I was lucky, I got a wire that a badly wanted fugitive was expecting mail at General Delivery, Blythe. This kind of stakeout could be a nightmare for a type A, just stand around for hours, maybe days. The PO opened at 9 and the subject appeared at 9:05. Nice guy, punctual. And a decent companion on the long drive. I was home by dinner, a rarity.

Sometimes the arrest was not so fortunate and timely.

One evening just as I was about to depart Blythe for home I got a teletype that a fugitive who had been indicted for Interstate Transportation of Stolen Property had listed a Blythe address. Details were scant but such an ITSP indictment should only issue for fairly serious serial bad checks. The teletype could not be ignored and I wasn't due to return for a month.

The address was a small old bungalow well out of town, modest by even local standards. In Blythe radiators were regarded as lawn trolls. Again book procedure would be to check the neighbors and call for backup. Again I just banged on the door.

The door was opened by the nicest old codger one could hope to meet. He kindly invited me in to meet "mother" who offered coffee and homemade cookies. I identified myself and my mission and he acknowledged to our mutual surprise that he was the person named in the warrant, name, rank and serial number, no question about it.

I knew immediately something was wrong but had no alternative. I arrested him, read him his rights, handcuffed him, heaven help me, and led him out to the car. The old folks continued befuddled but helpful. "Mother" packed us some cookies.

During the long drive to Riverside it became more and more evident that if this guy was a bad check artist then Mother Teresa was a mugger. His callused hands were strangers to fountain pens. He had done minor time in his youth but had never written a check of any kind and had never been out of the state.

We arrived much too late for a hearing so he had to spend the night in jail. First thing in the morning I got him to a hearing, released on recognizance and back on a bus for Blythe. What a mess.

A major strength and a major weakness of the Bureau were an insistence on channels. This preserves documentation but hinders communication. Indictment and recognizance are judicial procedures, supposedly removed from the realm of the investigator but often manipulated by him for better or worse. I knew the codger could not possibly be guilty but I could not document this and in the due course of time the machinery would grind him expensively to trial in Colorado.

A series of bad interstate checks had surfaced in Colorado and were routinely submitted to the vaunted FBI Lab where they uncharacteristically opined there were similarities with the limited handwriting on the ages old fingerprint cards of the almost illiterate old timer. Some idiot agent took the foto from the card around and got some idents (I guarantee you can get idents of a foto of a gorilla) and took this whole silly package to the grand jury. Ridiculous. But I challenge the reader to compose a document stating that in spite of the FBI Lab and the Idents and the Grand Jury this dude could not possibly be responsible. And my supervisors challenged my efforts.

It was months and mountains of paper before the indictment was quashed but the codger suffered no more.

No lawyers were involved and none in Blythe was the wiser, not that a little jail time was any barrier to social acceptance in Blythe.

Usually the clang of a jail door was a very satisfying sound to my ears, signifying a resolution of a social problem. Not this time. I still feel terrible about putting those fine old folks through that ordeal. "Mother" must have spent a gawdawful night.

Had no compunction about scarfing those cookies though. It was a very long day.

Grand Juries and indictments evolved to protect the citizenry from unjust accusations by overzealous police. The few times I was involved in bad arrests it was the conscientious investigator who provided the protection.

The Great Train Escape

Naturally we lived on the wrong side of the tracks in Indio and a daily inconvenience could be the sometimes tedious wait in the broiling sun while a train was in the station. One could see the passengers peering out from their cool steel cabins like space travelers pausing on the moon.

One night the train carried some very dangerous men. Two men, convicted of murder in Florida in unrelated cases, had been found in custody in California. The thrifty Floridians had sent one elderly courthouse loafer out to see Disneyland and escort these killers home. I later learned that the officers in LA had been horrified to turn these murderers over to this lone bumbler. I later learned that LA officers would have been horrified at a lot of stuff that passed for police work in Florida.

They were all escorted to the wonderful Los Angeles depot and put aboard a compartment bound for Florida. The marshal from the mangroves had two pairs of handcuffs, two pistols and a bottle of whisky. He cuffed up the killers, put his guns under his pillow and bedded down with his bottle. As soon as he was zonked they jumped him, unlocked the cuffs, tied him up, tucked the pistols under their belts and got off at Indio. Probably celebrated with a shot of Jack Black.

It was some hours before the conductor found the cracker, and news of the escape got back to Indio. We organized a huge manhunt but it soon became clear that two real desperados had gotten clean away and were probably already sticking up gas stations in Texas. Unlawful Flight to Avoid Confinement-Murder times two. Big cases, and nightmare cases for the case agent, me, because there were no logical leads in my area.

What was one to do? Put out an APB! An All Points Bulletin, that's the ticket. California had a wonderful police teletype network but it was abused to the point of uselessness. Thousands of teletypes nattering away the night grinding out yards of APBs that no one ever read. Police placebos. Don't worry Miz Smith we got an APB out on that sucker.

One of the beauties of criminal work was that there was every possibility of reaching a productive, positive end result. Fat chance of that. I was looking at two major cases that would probably dog me to the end of my days. Fugitive cases required monthly evidence of efforts to locate. These guys had almost certainly split and returned to Florida.

Then by golly one night Pat Cunningham called. Pat was Chief of Police in Indio, wonderful old man, hewn of granite. They had some old rummy in the drunk tank with an interesting tale. He had been staying in a hobo jungle way out under the tamarisks. He and his fellow vagabonds were sitting around toasting 'smores and exchanging campfire stories. One of the wanderers spun a wild tale of overpowering a lawman and jumping from a train.

We gathered a posse and rode out of town. Armed murderers assaulting an officer and escaping get a lot of attention in law enforcement circles. Auras of adrenaline were swirling around the shotgun muzzles as we surrounded the grove.

We lined them up and sorted them out and sure enough, there was our man. He gave us no trouble. Actually he was just a drifter who had gunned down someone in a barroom brawl, a bad C & W ballad. He had been riding the rails and had no idea he had returned to the area of the escape. He was terrified of his companion who was a real thug and who had jumped and thumped the deputy. They had separated right after the escape.

The cracker copper could have been killed and gotten others killed. He should have been prosecuted.

Me and Hoover Meet Again

Meeting Hoover was always a huge production, choreographed by Kafka, designed to terrify. Who knows why. He thought FBI meant Feudal Barony Inviolate. At the end of training school we were paraded by him in a procedure that had all our counselors petrified. Any goofup and they were gone.

Our second meeting was even less agreeable.

We had spent a couple of years in Indio and it was time to pay the piper. The price of admission to Spanish School was a two-year tour in Puerto Rico and our turn had come.

Jurisdiction for the Indio Resident Agency had passed from San Diego to Los Angeles, unnoticed by the Times. No particular difference, except now I went in to LA every month. Technically the Assistant Special Agent in Charge (ASAC), a demi deity, was in charge of the RAs, but my actual boss was the stolen car supervisor. The ASAC had left several messages for me to report myself but what with one thing and another the opportunity hadn't prospered.

In those days it was all but impossible to get from Indio to Puerto Rico. By now we had another golden-haired girl and a boy, making four children under six years of age. Tacky. Travel arrangements were a nightmare. We sold the house at a substantial loss, forwarded our few pathetic sticks of furniture and the distraught DG and kids were with her folks in Arizona.

I remained behind to close the office, clean up all the details, turn in all the materials at Los Angeles, and then take a train to Arizona, pick up the oldest girl and the car, overland to New Orleans to ship the car and then fly to San Juan.

These delicate arrangements were graven in granite.

My last night there was yet another late call from the Indio PD. They had a young couple in custody and felt it was a federal matter. It was federalíssimo. This kid had escaped from federal prison, stolen and transported several cars, kidnaped this juvenile female, violated her and rented her out, he had broken every federal statute on the books, a walking Title 18. The funny thing was he wasn't a bad kid. However the girl, the victim, was a holy terror, a violent runaway nut case.

So it's up all night with this pair taking their complex statements, and then transporting them to hearings and custody in Riverside, and then on into Los Angeles, where I have to finish the paper work and make the 2 o'clock train.

As part of the travel scheme I had forwarded most of my clothes, leaving out only one faded cotton suit that Gabby Hayes wouldn't have worn to the funeral of a junk yard dog. My plan was to wear this one final day and then discard it. When I discard clothing it is no longer suitable for a rag rug at an ice rink. I had worn this suit under heat and pressure all night and all day.

At that time the LA office consisted of a huge bullpen surrounded by the supervisors' offices. Normally the place looked like Grand Central Station, scores of bustling, hustling bodies. Now, not a soul. Something was wrong but I had no time. Nobody said anything to me, nobody knew me.

Here is this unshaven, smelly, disheveled youth wearing what appear to be pajamas right in the middle of this huge, empty squadroom, pounding the bejesus out of a typewriter.

Out of the corner of my eye I could see a small group moving around the periphery of the room in which seemed to be a ceremonial pattern. I had already begun to suspect that this was one of Hoover's annual inspection trips, which coincided with the Del Mar races, since Hoover took no holidays.

Another Hooverian bugaboo was that agents should be on the streets and there were endless forms to document this lie. Therefore on his rare visits to a field office all the agents were chased out on the streets.

Suddenly a hand intruded into the space over my typewriter and its owner acknowledged himself to be J. Edgar Hoover. I had the presence of mind to allow that this was certainly a great honor without offering any personal particulars. Another hand was identified as attached to Clyde Tolson. Hovering and glowering in the background was the ASAC, the host of this party and my nominal boss. He had no idea as to the identity of this ill-clothed apparition and he is furious because he had ordered the place vacated.

The group moved on and I resumed my report. I can only assume that they supposed this was some scruffy informant turning in a secret report before disappearing into the ground.

The report was completed, I made the train, car, boat, and plane connections. The GHG got registered in the first grade. The suit was spurned by the Sally Army.

This may be the only time Hoover ever actually saw a field agent in the heat of action.

The Rich Port

Puerto Rico was an awful jolt at first. It was blazing hot, a tropical sauna far more punishing than the dry desert furnace. The people were speaking some language seemingly unrelated to what we had studied. Housing was unavailable. There were no real supermarkets or department stores. Driving was dramatic and disorder was off the scale. The office was staffed with colorful misfits. I very nearly packed it in.

But we grew to love the place, in part because of its overpowering tropicality. I finally found a small house by pounding the streets. The people were friendly, the natives and especially the gringos, in the neighborhood and in the office. Something about being castaways drew us together.

There were parties nearly every night, real parties, always with dancing, drinking, flirting, singing, games, not at all the diplomatic do-si-dos of later years overseas. We had access to the many military bases, with excellent schools and recreational facilities, a huge bonus. There was a 15% pay premium so we even had a few bucks. We even had help, a lilting lady known throughout the community as the black Kim Novak.

Surprisingly the work was no particular strain. People were usually extraordinarily helpful. Again I had the good fortune to be assigned to the criminal squad. Security work there was a nightmare, concerned mostly with the volatile and nutty nationalistas. The office was located in a treasure of a deco building in the heart of Old San Juan, one of the great pedestrian precincts of the world, cobbled calles leading past arcaded shops and ancient churches to the magnificent fortress. Still thrills me. But don't hang around much after dark.

The office was staffed with eccentrics, no sensible suit would put in for this post. The Agent in Charge was a miserable prick but that was nothing new. He headed the more prestigious Security Squad and sent the more bizarre rejects upstairs to the Criminal Squad under the charge of his fawning Assistant.

There were great little restaurants serving the local specialty, rice and beans and whatever died recently. Weekends were fabulous, tennis and volleyball and snorkeling, crystal water and sailing to deserted white sand islets, hot Caribe rhythms in the balmy evenings at the O clubs.

I am sometimes surprised we ever opted to leave.

The Death of a Criminal Informant

I told you I had never killed anyone. That was a lie. We were only beginning to get acquainted, you and I.

Upon arrival in San Juan not only did I have the good fortune to be assigned to the criminal squad, I was also assigned a fully qualified criminal informant, not a creature one encountered in a casual afternoon stroll. Criminal Informants (CIs) were a huge deal. Hoover was convinced they were the key to successful investigations and even claimed to have developed one himself, a madam in Ciudad Juárez, Mexico. Chure. Jota Edgair jew mus not come here again, that red satin frock ees too flashy.

Point is CIs were big stuff and as always Hoover tried to formalize the process, like peanut butter sales charts. Everyone had to have several PCIs (Potential Criminal Informants) and record TOPCI (Time Spent on PCIs) daily. Seriously. Basically we were required to commit FAG (Fraud Against the Government) daily. The Bureau was hell on the very Boy Scouts it sought to attract.

This CI had been developed and qualified by an agent under transfer. In the usual press of time there had been no opportunity to meet this gem personally, although, of course, the record would show that this manual requirement had been met. All manual requirements were met. Punto.

I couldn't wait to burrow into the files of my new prize. This guy was a wonder, he had turned up fugitives, suspects, stolen property, bent politicos, nacionalistas, the whole nueve yardas. Dinamita.

Informants' files were kept under special security to further cloak their identities. Turned out this guy ran a little grocery, a colmado, deep in one of the swampy barrios. Man he knew everything that moved in that barrio. He lived above the colmado and never left the premises. Better and better. None of this skulking around dark alleys in the night and exchanging paroles and passwords and packages. Nothing strange about a gringo dropping in on a colmado.

So I set out to meet this jewel, who the record showed I had already met. Encantado. Mucho gusto. Servidor.

Most addresses in the barrios were not terribly helpful. A typical address would be Parada 18, the nearest bus stop. But this was very specific. The corner of Calle Equis and Avenida Ygriega in the Barrio Almas Podridas. There was such a barrio and such an intersection, but no colmado. There couldn't be a mistake. The colmado had some characteristic highblown name like "El Garañon Galante" (The Attentive Stud Camel.) No joy, nothing there.

It began to be clear that this was an imaginary informant, a phantom figment of a fevered mind. Someone, at wit's end to meet the demands for informants, had started down the primrose path. It was easy at first, make up some Fulano de Tal, a few sly meetings, a nudge and a wink. Then start to attribute info to him, easy enough, culled from the papers or police or your own investigations. No sweat. Find a violator, which we all did all the time. Then report that Fulano shopped him. Lookin' good.

Then a transfer. What to do? He can't tell the supervisor or trust the new guy. Maybe it will all go away. So he just departed. Now the dilemma is mine. If I blow the whistle several careers are in the toilet.

I don't have the eggs to maintain this charade for two years and then dump it on some other dummy.

What did I do? What could I do? I killed him.

Even now it is painful to recall. Wet work is no piquenique in the parque. One bright, balmy morning, the record will show, his body was found in the colmado. Death by cause or causes unknown. Who knows, ¿quién sabe? It was a bad neighborhood and he was playing a dangerous game.

The criminal supervisor, a fervent player of the Bureau's games, was the most deeply distressed of all the mourners. This was the best damned CI in the office. Now he was gone, as surely as the supervisor would have been gone had I blown the whistle.

Well it was up to me to come up with a suitable replacement. In spite of considerable pressure I just couldn't do it, couldn't raise another fatted calf for the county fair and then sacrifice him.

But I began to wish I had let him live. He wasn't hurting anyone and he made the hierarchy happy.

Lookie Lookie Lookie

Bureau policy was to work solo, much more efficient and more to my taste. But policy also required two agents for many situations, especially apprehensions. Since apprehensions were always a possibility we worked tandem a lot. The unwritten code was never to refuse a request for help, which could be a severe test in San Juan because some of these guys were looney tunes.

Cuentas wasn't looney, more like eccentric. He was heart of gold and popular because he really knew the island and was the only one who actually spoke Puerto Rican. He actually did a lot of good investigation, little of which appeared on paper, the exact opposite of most of the rest who did little work but put up a barrage of paper. But everything he touched turned to ca ca.

Our office overlooked the beautiful bay where often Navy seaplanes could be seen painting their biwordly arabesques. There was always a picturesque row of goletas, sailing schooners, which serviced the smaller islands, moored at the quay, living artifacts. The crews were suitably piratical and Cuentas wanted help in arresting one. We wouldn't even have to check out a car, just stroll down, grab the guy and waltz him over to the historical Princesa prison. Piece of pastel.

The charge was Theft from Interstate Shipment (TFIS). Of course, everyone on the docks was involved in TFIS. Even the watchmen were involved in TFIS even as they were watchmaneando. (Actual verb, typical Caribespeak.)

Routine, I barely glanced at the paper. Cuentas had good information from his good sources that the cook on the goleta "Pinche Puta" was dealing in TFIS and had gotten authority from the U.S. Attorney to go to the U.S. Commissioner for a warrant, all very correct. In the case the warrant was issued for Unknown Subject (UNSUB) (meaning the true name was not known) aka (also known as) "Cookie".

We strolled down to the Puta and asked for "Cookie". A surprisingly young man appeared and acknowledges that he was indeed "Cookie". We duly arrested and Mirandized him but something was clearly podrido en Dinamarca. This agreeable youth did not fit the image of the notorious dock thief we sought. After some hassle we arranged to quash the warrant and release our friend, none the worse.

Cuentas had neglected to allow for the fact that every goleta had a cook and they were interchangeable as anchors and generically known as "Cookie".

The case against Cookie crumbled.

Shooting the Bull

Brahma was an agent from New York City, meaning he had an attitude and a half and couldn't drive. He was from a Spanish background and spoke fluent street Spanish but couldn't write it. I was a wizard at written Spanish but couldn't speak it. When we took statements in Spanish it was the deaf leading the blind.

Because of his aggressiveness and command of the language he could be quite effective on the streets. But few wanted to travel with him. He demanded to be behind the wheel and he was a terror, cursing and screaming and banging the horn. Even worse once he got it started. He was, seriously, thrown out of his car pool. With prejudice. A menace.

Through one of his sources he got a lead on the whereabouts of one of my fugitives, hiding in the hills above Utuado. I wanted this guy badly and the price was cutting the bull in on the bust. So we head out, Brahma driving naturally.

As we drove by the Navy base he turned in and parked at the Chiefs' club, renowned like all such for its chow. "Hey, we gotta eat don't we." The Bull was obviously well known at the venue and first thing I know he is in a shuffleboard tournament. Finally I literally drug him away, already two hours tardy by my timepiece. No problem, says B., make it up on the road.

Two hours of terror brought us to the edge of a big reservoir. The fugitive lives on the far side, no roads. No choice but to hire a boatman. Two more hours of terror crossing a windy lake in a leaky rowboat and the nearest life preserver is on the wall of the Chiefs' Club bearing their motto "We take care of our own." At least Brahma doesn't row.

There was no problem locating and collaring the fugitive but we are far from home. If he so much as stood up in the boat we're all dead. It was getting late. It was the cutting season. Backroads in Puerto Rican cane country were notorious in cutting season, huge overloaded heedless speeding trucks around every bend of the narrow lanes.

Brahma is at the wheel, anxious to get back to the tournament. The fugitive and I are petrified.

I asked him to slow down, I demanded he slow down, I asked for the con, I demanded control. Finally I told him if he didn't turn the wheel over to me I was going to pull my pistol and shoot him dead.

He knew I meant it. Something in my voice convinced him. Something that said I had killed before to survive.

El Aeropuerto

Ever since I was a kid I have loved airports. Exciting places, high energy, high risk, frantic activity, the dynamics of travel, adrenal ducts in overdrive. There are great people working in airports, special people, caught up in the frenzy.

An airport is a satellite, self-contained, almost independent of earth. Airport people are a special fraternity, with their own language, signals, codes, passwords. There are hidden passageways, concealed observation ports, all a secret policeman could wish for, and even in those pre-skyjacking times FBI agents were given a parole to enter this special world.

Good thing I liked airports because I spent a lot of time at them. In San Juan we lived near the airport and I caught most of the calls. The Pan Am manager was a neighbor and dear friend. In those days a Pan Am manager was a deity just under and to the right of whoever was caudillo.

Jets were just making their appearance. I loved them, so graceful and beautiful. But they multiplied the dynamics. Picking out a fugitive or suspect arriving on a DC-3 was easy. But hundreds of people boiled off these jets, each with a story.

Whole Lotto Stuff Going On

B.O. was another of our resident flakes and self-appointed scourge of the lottery traffickers. Lottery was legal in Puerto Rico but not so the other nearby islands under our splendid flag. The "Billetes" chant was the national anthem of Puerto Rico, but lottery was illegal in the Virgin Islands, and contraband tickets were therefore illegal and profitable.

I hated these cases. The traffickers were housewives, often as not, and rarely prosecuted. The seizures were a terrible headache, tedious days to inventory and double-check, any one of these babies could be the big enchilada.

One afternoon B.O. frantically assembled all hands to fall on the airport. A little Douglas DC-3 was even then warming up on the tarmac and he had ironclad info that everyone aboard was transporting tickets. So we had the flight stopped and climbed aboard.

Sure enough every single passenger was carrying a stack of lottery tickets. It was going to be a long afternoon. Now one of the passengers happened to be a priest, frocked out in full Roman regalia. We took name, rank and serial numbers and the tickets. But B.O., who was known to be a notorious RC as were so many of the boyos of those days, gave the priest absolution and sent him on his way.

Tit for tat? You scratch my back and I'll see you in paradise. Corruption is clothed in many costumes.

It was an ugly lesson for the Mormon kids.

Cuchi Cuchi Cuchillo

Another big caper at the San Juan International Airport.

The airport police called me that they had a suspect in custody who might be of interest. This turned out to be a kid from the Big Apple visiting his homeland for the first time. He had come swaggering through the airport with his bopping, Bronx bravado and the locals naturally pulled him over to the curb. I'm convinced that half of the police problems in the world are due to bored cops. They sign up expecting gangbusters and spend the next twenty years watching linoleum wear out.

They stopped the kid and shook him down and to their astonishment found no dope. But the kid was giving his Cagney you coppers got nuttin on me routine so they dug some more. And found a switchblade knife. Now transporting an attitude interstate was unfortunately not federal but the switch blade knife act had just been signed into law. In fact this might have been the first case.

Some Assistant United States Attorney who thought this might serve as a healthy and historic precedent and a feather in his cap for being first, authorized the filing of a complaint.

So I took custody and escorted the now subdued kid and his knife downtown to the offices of dear deaf old Commissioner Julia. His job was to insure that there was probable cause and in his usual courteous and highly conscientious fashion he asked to see the knife.

It was big and ugly like all switchblades but old and rusty, nothing so grand as the OJ number.

The U.S. Commissioner then asked to see action demonstrated. The switch was activated and the blade was released. But the knife was weary and the blade was a bit shy about revealing itself in such circumstances. Instead of snapping savagely and menacingly erect, it creaked slowly out of the case and gave up entirely after opening about an inch. It would not have presented peril to a pistachio.

This would have been a humiliation to the kid in the streets but resulted in a humiliation to me in federal court.

Commissioner Julia promptly and rightfully quashed the proceedings, and another arch criminal walked free.

A little WD-40 and it would have been the slammer.

The Luminescent Limo

Extortion was a popular crime in Puerto Rico. A very disagreeable crime. Typical would be an anonymous note to a prominent family threatening the children unless there is a payoff. Usually the demand specifies no notification of police and a convoluted payoff plan follows. The Bureau has a remarkable record in these cases.

They are very tough cases, high priority, high pressure, short time frame, and always the fear for the victims. This was exacerbated by Hoover's demand for zero failure. It is damn easy to sit in a fancy office far from the scene surrounded by sycophants and demand flawless performance, especially without any useful direction or field experience. Witness General Eisenhower.

This case was typical. A prominent family, very decent, responsible people, not that that should be a factor. A note, a demand, a complicated payoff. Extortionists spend years pacing penal yards planning perfect payoffs.

The Chief, José Satanás, took personal charge and there were the usual endless conferences and consultations. Finally the night of the payoff.

Following instructions the sturdy matriarch of the family was driven in the family limo down a prescribed series of dark lanes. Joe Huevo, quite a fine young agent, had volunteered to be in the back seat with the package.

The package supposedly contained unmarked bills but actually was stuffed with detection powder, bright, violent violet, fluorescent, permeating, permanent stain dye, the latest thing.

Upon the proper signal Joe was supposed to heave the package and follow it soon after gun in hand. I did not volunteer for this assignment. The rest of us were posted, hopefully unnoticed, all around the countryside, watching and waiting.

We could see the limo slowly approaching the target area. The tail car, commanded by Satanás himself, was supposed to follow at a discreet distance. But as we could see it was practically on top of the limo, might as well use a tow chain and save gas. Satanás was going to insure that there would be no misfire on the payoff because there would be no payoff, not with that coverage. We were furious, all that effort for nothing.

Who knows what the family thought. There was a lot of blind faith in the FBI in those days. The chauffeur called me plaintively the next day. The dove grey upholstery of the Caddy limo was now splotchy violet and nothing seemed to cleanse it. Of course not, that was the point. I called the Lab but they were of no help, they worked years to make this stuff indelible.

Joe Huevo, who carried a pair of huevos, looked like terminal impetigo for a few weeks. I think he got a commendation but his wife wouldn't go near him.

The Commissioner

The U.S. Commissioner acted in lieu of a federal judge, safeguarding procedures preliminary to prosecution. Commissioner Julia was the most courteous and courtly man you could want to meet. He was always punctiliously correct and immaculately dressed. In a white linen suit of course. Amazingly one could find such fine gentlemen throughout the Latin tropics. The actor Raul Julia was probably from the same family, had the same dignified, agreeably deranged air.

He was the only Commissioner on the island and I had to consult with him almost daily. He was always gracious and attentive and I wanted to kill him. When Resident Agents needed an arrest warrant I ran the paper by Julia. This was a lot of paper. He had no secretary or command of touch typing so I spent agonizing hours in his stifling office while he carefully ground out this boilerplate.

Once I needed a search warrant. There was good information that a local employee of the Post Exchange had a porch full of refrigerators. There was a lot of Crime on Government Reservation (CGR) cases involving the exchanges. So I sought a search warrant. Officers must not be permitted to ransack willy nilly a man's castle. This was my first so I reviewed the Commissioner's files.

Every single search warrant form bore the name of one single agent. Mad Dog Murphy. Murphy was a very eager agent. His wife said, hell don't bother to pay him, just give him a badge and a gun. There was no reason for the commissioner to consider this strange. I was the arrest warrant gringo and Murph was the search warrant gringo.

But I was riding the criminal desk much of the time and I knew from a regular review of all the criminal files that there was no paper trail or product from all these searches.

I was hesitant to research further because I feared that the confidential source on whose information the warrants were issued was the imaginary informant I had just killed.

There weren't any refrigerators on the porch either.

Adiós Puerto Rico

The two-year contract passed all too fast. It was very tempting to sign over. It was a nice life style. Loads of friends, fabulous schools for the kids, wonderful weekends, interesting work, constant parties, household help, even some savings, beautiful place, great food, distinctly not Ponca City.

Puerto Rico had great food everywhere but the restaurants. Most of the office ate every meal at the dreadful U.S. style coffee shop across the street. While even down on the docks the longshoremen were downing buckets of fabulous arroz con habichuelas (rice and red beans). Another specialty was arroz con pollo (rice and chicken) which Cuentas always served when there was a catastrophe in the chicken yard. The ubiquitous wonderful rice was cooked in a special heavy kettle. First onions were braised in sofrito, lard and achiote (annato), low rent saffron.

The frequent festivals featured lechón asado (spit-roasted pig, with honored guests offered the ears. Bacalao, dried salt cod was a huge local favorite. Latin lutfiske, awful. But bacalaitos, cod fritters cooked in hot fat, irresistible. Pan de Agua, no-fat baguettes, were home delivered nightly. They turned to rock in an hour but never lasted that long.

Our favorite place was Mario's, a nearby thatched hut on the beach. Even had a pianist who played in a captivating syncopated Latino style, hoppin Jesus Joplin. The place featured asopao de jueyes. Neither of these words appear in any of my Spanish dictionaries. Asopao is rice stew, a soupy paella. Jueyes are land crabs, God's most hideous creation, hunchbacked lobsters from hell, which lurched across the highways at night attacking teenagers. Wonderful meat, once purged.

Tampa Tales

For a variety of reasons we opted to return to the mainland after two years in Puerto Rico. My liver was one reason. There was a legend that one was given some consideration for an office of preference after a tour on the island but it never happened in my time. Shortly before our transfer some friends had finished their tours. One couple was Floridian, and listed the three Florida offices. The others were Texans and listed the three Texas offices. All these offices needed Spanish speakers. Yes, the wires were crossed. What was the point of two unhappy families far from home? Serious stuff. A divorce in one family, a suicide in the other. Happy Mr. Hoover?

Shortly before Satanás, the sadistic Agent in Charge, had been transferred to Tampa. Upon departure I was foolish enough to tell him I hoped to God I would never have to work under him again. We of course had listed Western offices.

Tampa was a small office, maybe 50 men, recently upgraded from a Resident Agency. Just in time, all hell was breaking loose. There was a large Cuban colony violently polarized by the Castro situation, there was the Ragsdale Armored Car job, biggest since Brinks, there was Santos Trafficante just as the Bureau was finally taking action on the Mafia, we had bank robberies, Top Ten fugitives, stuff breaking daily.

I was assigned to the Security squad, work I hated, under Satanás, a man I despised. I was never home, the schools were lousy in both senses, it was a horrible year.

Ybor City

Security work meant informants. Security work in Tampa meant Cubans. Cubans meant Ybor City. I hated security and informants and was ambivalent about Tampa, Cubans and work but I loved Ybor City. This was the heart of the Cuban colony, once removed from Havana, twice removed from Spain. It reeked with ambiente, world class restaurants, great snack bars, superb cigars and coffee, the old Spanish clubs, the latin rhythms and the dominos clattering counterpoint. Definitely Ybor City, not Ponca City.

This was the early years of Castro and the colony was bitterly and deeply divided. Close-knit families were losing cousins on both sides. Informants, so difficult to cultivate on the criminal side, were lined up at the door. Strike that, queues are not credible in a Cuban context.

Another communications gap. I was assigned to contact a Cuban university professor and never understood a word she said and she never stopped talking. Back to the ABCs, which in Cuban are ano, burro and coño.

I was assigned an organization known as the Fair Play for Cuba (FPCC), which gained considerable fame when Lee Harvey Oswald joined it rather than the Elks (BPOE). Along with the FPCC was a list of several dozen names. Your job, should you choose to accept it, was to characterize the FPCC and identify the members. Not a walk in the park for a neophyte, especially with Profesora Charo spitting gibberish in his ear. Everybody in Ybor was quick to identify the FPCC as a bunch of commie rats, but this was of little help to the Attorney General when he got up in the morning in the mood to anathemize.

It was a big job to sort out and identify all these players.

This was complicated by the idiosyncrasies of the Spanish surnames. There aren't that many of them in sunny Castile and far too many in the tropics. All around the Caribe there are a lot of peculiar, patchwork, artsy-craftsy names, due to the gallantry of seafarers of yore, phonetic miscalculations and the natural lyricism that lushly flourishes under the trades.

Bonapart Rosabelt was one so blessed. Or rather two. Bonapart was identified by several sources as a fat, old grocer in Ybor who was a flaming red Fidelista, officer in the FPCC. Put him on the list. But turns out there are two Bonapart Rosabelts, both fat grocers in Ybor, but only one followed Fidel. This was far harder to correct than false arrests, particularly since Satanás' mad distribution policies had copies to everyone but the Coast Guard Auxiliary in Anchorage.

We were supposed to get fotos of all these folks. Washington sent out a special camera concealed in a briefcase, real spook stuff, but these folks wouldn't pose. Another misplaced criminal agent perfected the technique. He would lure the subjects out of their shops by slurring their manhood and then point and shoot the briefcase. Worked a treat. Got all these great shots of enraged Cubans screaming and waving cigars.

This was right in the middle of the Bay of Pigs. This was top level, we were not supposed to discuss it even among ourselves. Every little bebé in the barrio knew that the CIA was recruiting and training Cubans for an invasion. There was enormous excitement. Uncle Sam wouldn't venture such a stunt without the certainty of success.

Fidel would fall. Bet on it.

One More for Ybor

One day we were assigned to track some Bulgarian diplomats who were vacationing in Florida. This security surveillance stuff was all new to me. Surveillance can be a horror. It takes a lot of people and equipment to do properly, resources that are rarely available. I could weep when I see Tommy Lee Jones calling up all those choppers. Don't get made and don't lose them were the standard, helpful Bureau instructions, all but impossible. Impossible standards necessarily lead to a lot of fudging.

We picked up the surveillance baton from a team that had trailed the Bulgies from Jacksonville. To my astonishment I found that we were tracking these people practically bumper to bumper, no pretense at finesse. I have no idea as to the antecedents of this exercise in futility. The cables carried no such instructions. The senior agents seemed perfectly content with the arrangement. It was certainly unlikely that they were going to engage in any significant activity with this coverage.

It was another game with unwritten, unspoken ground rules, played for years, still scoreless.

At one point our friends began circling and it was apparent that they were looking for famed Ybor City and were lost.

Finally one of the senior agents got out and showed them the way.

Take <u>that</u> you commie rats. <u>That</u> road.

Santos Trafficante

One of the really great names. "Pious Promoter" might be an acceptable translation and description. He was supposed to be the mob's main man in Florida. Hoover had denied the existence of the Mafia for decades, the critical decades when they gained power and corrupted our major cities. We are still playing catch-up and never did catch up to Santos.

I have no idea why Hoover chose not to pursue organized crime. His apologists claim it was the lack of statutory authority, but that never deterred him in the security field. I think he avoided it, as he did narcotics, because it was costly, complex and conducive to corruption.

After Apalachin it was apparent that there was a nationwide crime syndicate and the Justice Department began to shove Hoover's nose into the mess. We were sicked on Santos.

Now we were literally trying to catch up to Santos, pounding across the highways of Central Florida at 120 MPH. We were driving a sleek new Plymouth Golden Commando, the newest and hottest car in the office. Naturally it was assigned to Satanás who never left the office, but he lent out his pet for the occasional run to clean out the carbon.

We had surveillance on Santos and for once were doing it right, two cars intermittently leapfrogging. For once he might not know we were around and lead us to something more interesting than the Knights of Columbus.

Santos suddenly headed north out of town and put on a turn of speed. Very interesting. Gotcha covered.

We were a couple of comfortable miles back when the lead car radioed that "Atlas" was turning west on State Highway 24. We professionals used code names like "Atlas" to confound the target. He probably had a receiver and might be listening. He could have heard about the turn but he knew his name wasn't Atlas. Pretty slick stuff.

So when we got up to the intersection with highway 24 we duly turned west. After a bit we put on some speed to close the gap but we couldn't seem to raise the lead car visually or by radio. So we kicked in the afterburners. I figure we must have been going 130 when the engine blew.

We were hours getting back home. The chief was not pleased. He looked on that car as the favored child denied him in real life. He never saw it again.

It developed that the lead car, piloted by New Yorkers who favored the Florida offices for their declining years, had actually turned east but mistakenly messaged "west". A natural mistake since they have no sun to guide them on their home turf.

"Atlas" turned east to visit a relative in the state pen. If he was listening maybe he thought "East" was a code word too.

A decade later Santos would return to plague me in Costa Rica. Never did catch up with him. He caused me a lot more grief than I ever caused him.

Top Ten Tunes

The Bureau's Top Ten Fugitive program was a real attention grabber. A top tenner was a real coup. While I was in Chicago the cigars brought in tenners a couple of times and the whole office resonated with applause. But the publicity generates millions of false leads, which get tiresome quickly.

My partner and I helped track one to a motel in Tampa but naturally the cigars took over from us. The Assistant Special Agent in Charge (ASAC) took personal charge. On the way back to the office the subject started fumbling for his smokes and the ASAC went bananas and screamed for him to freeze. The subject calmly lit his 'ret and allowed that his captor seemed a tad nervous for this business.

Francisco "The Hook" Molina was the hottest fugitive in the business. He was a Castro thug who had killed some kid in a shootout. Reports of his whereabouts were coming out of the woodwork.

Someone notified FBI Miami that The Hook was even then boarding a DC-3 bound for Havana. Mad dog Murphy got the call. He sireened out on the runway, blocked the plane and started sorting through. The plane was loaded with diplomats but no Hook. However there was another fugitive aboard so Murphy got commended instead of fired.

In Tampa we got leads about The Hook all the time. The most elaborate scenario reported that he was going to meet with some Cuban gunboat way out in the Gulf. After many conferences a dozen heavily armed agents under the aforementioned ASAC boarded a Coast Guard cutter to cover the rendezvous.

To a layman landsman it seemed a horrendous problem but the calm young CG captain considered it a breeze. He could lay back over the horizon and close in when he detected the boats. All we had to do was pick out our fugitive.

That was easy enough, said the ASAC, the FBI had put out thousands of flyers with a full description. Hand me one a them flyers. Everyone started rummaging around. Several dozen armed men miles at sea on a dangerous mission to apprehend an international assassin. No flyers.

Now, knowing this ASAC, I knew this would happen and had squirreled away a bunch of these flyers in my parka. I savored the situation for a long l-o-n-g moment before producing the paper.

After a terrible gun battle we boarded the smoking hulk of the Cuban gunboat and were able to identify the charred remains of The Hook because of my flyers. Well, not really. Nothing happened, as I suspected. We spent a pleasant day at sea. Next life I'm joining the Coast Guard.

Actually I think we could have picked Francisco Molina even without the flyer. Right soon after we commanded "Hands Up". He wasn't called "The Hook" for nothing.

What! Time to Meet Hoover Again?

After a terrible year in Tampa I was scheduled for In Service training, regular professional updating and orientation in Washington and Quantico. This time I was to be trained as a firearms and defensive tactics instructor, quite to my taste.

Satanás wanted to know if I planned to see Hoover. I didn't think so, could see no advantage, although I was already in purgatory. He ordered me to see Hoover.

The first day in D.C. they ask right away if anyone wants to see Hoover, and everyone swivels their heads to see who the finks are. The guy next to me put up his hand and mine followed. We were the only ones and I swear I would never have done so without his lead. Our classmates became distant.

Later in the week we were summoned to the inner sanctum. There was a protocol to which I was a stranger. Genial small talk with the black doorkeeper. What do you mean there are no black agents? Fussy reminders from the secretaries, now be sure to take notes. And then about a half an hour with Hoover.

I didn't say 5 words. He rattled on and on about the Bureau and the commies and the crooks. He said some terrible things about Martin Luther King and Earl Warren. I just nodded and made hen scratches on the pad. I couldn't figure it out. This giant on the American scene rambling on for a half-hour or more to a nobody and he must do this several times a day, every day. I said nothing, asked for nothing, didn't even bother to mention we had met before. Finally he signaled the end and I returned to the glowering looks of my classmates.

As usual I enjoyed Quantico, summer camp with real firearms. The SAC, Wank Slow, was even wackier than the hierarchy in D.C. but he was rarely seen except on the far ranges blasting government birdshot into an innocent sky. Slow made the usual introductory lecture, stressing safety and especially noting that there had never been a firearms accident at Quantico, which we all knew to be an outrageous untruth.

Slow also described a new firearms course. An electronic marvel where you went against a fast gun on the screen. This was to be done on free time and sign up fast because it was very popular. I couldn't wait because Quantico was pretty boring in the evening now that ping-pong was proscribed. I searched and searched and finally found a dustcovered machine in the basement. It didn't work. Never had. Nobody told Slow. Or maybe they did. No one else even bothered to look.

I did well on the courses and they were considering me for the staff, a very inviting advancement over Tampa, counselor at the Boy Scout camp.

The last day I was called to Slow's office. Slow was seething. What now? He handed me a sealed envelope with the comment that I knew damned well what it was about. It was a letter of transfer to Mexico City, my number one office of preference, the impossible dream.

Never did figure out why this outraged Slow. He probably thought I was one of those slimy finks who weasel their way into Hoover's ephemeral grace in order to wheedle a choice assignment. His own career in a word. But even a mule would have the manners to offer good wishes.

México Lindo

Mexico. It sounded too exotic to even be on the same planet as Ponca City. We had heard of the Mexico City office. It seemed a dream assignment but unattainable. True, I went to Spanish school, but that was to get out of Chicago. True, we listed Mexico as our first preference, but that was a two-edged sword.

We sold the house, nice little house but lost everything we had saved in Puerto Rico. We bought a huge tin trunk and loaded it on the roof rack. Feared the whole trip it would plunge through and kill us all. The four little kids are crouched fearfully in the back. Where are the crazy big people taking us now.

We had a nice trip, all along the Gulf Coast through New Orleans and into legendary Laredo. There it was. Mexico. Right across the creek. We plunged in the next day. Cleared customs in an hour or so with the help of a gratificación (bribe, what a great language). Motored on down to the capital where we were met and escorted to a luxury apartment hotel, paid for by Tio Sam.

We were right in the heart of town, a wonder-filled market across the street. People all fussed over the kids, who were in heaven. A huge silver peso coin (8 cents US) bought all kinds of goodies.

We all loved it from the first day, fabulous place, fabulous people.

Dangereuse Foreign Liaison

What in the world is the FBI doing overseas, one might well ask. Actually there was an aura of spook city about overseas operations dating back to WW Dos when Hoover sent agents to Latin America to check on the Nazis. An FBI presence was still delicate from a sovereignty standpoint and our indoctrination was to avoid this identification. To the point that the kids would quietly turn the channel if an FBI program appeared. But it was all perfectly legal and we didn't carry any badges or stinking guns.

Host countries were glad to have us. We helped clear up cases of questionable Americans and Latin America was lousy with such. It behooved both countries to have investigations progress in an orderly fashion, there had been too many chaotic cowboy operations.

There were ample general investigative leads, kidnapings, murder, extortion, fraud, skyjacking, car-rings, stuff breaking all the time. A high priority was the return of fugitives, who were forever trying to find haven South of the Border. Extradition was hopeless, there was not a single successful extradition either way in my 20 years.

It's no good saying this work could have been done through correspondence or diplomatic channels. Nothing would ever get accomplished. Mexico and the U.S. both suffer from a multiplicity of police agencies, all with their own agendas. We were in contact with dozens of such agencies, shepherding the leads. I am amazed at how much we got done.

And it was fun. Many of the cases were exciting and challenging and the results could be dramatic and rewarding. Arrests, deportations, recoveries, prosecutions, the world was a better place. Just hitting those ancient bricks in that fascinating city and dealing with those colorful people was a daily delight.

But first I had to spend another apprenticeship on the security side. Sigh.

The American Communist Group in Mexico (ACGM)

For my first tour in Mexico my penance was serving on the security squad, mostly working the American Communist Group in Mexico, the infamous ACGM. Sounds ominous doesn't it? At one time there were several men on this assignment. Man we had them commie rats covered like a blanket. A slight problem was there was no such thing as the ACGM. The ACGM was an invention by my predecessors for convenience in reporting. An organization so secret its very existence was unknown to the membership.

Oh there were a lot of American Communists residing in Mexico and they had a loose social association, but that was about it. After all the McCarthy and Hollywood Ten hoopla quite a few gringo reds moved to Mexico, traditionally hospitable to refugee reds. They claimed to be fleeing prosecution. Decades earlier old Gus Hall, bless his sturdy Stalinist heart, had been booted out of Mexico by a rightist regime but that was about it prosecution-wise.

McCarthy was abominable but there is no question that most of these folks were absolutely dedicated to the overthrow of the American system and the installation of Soviet Communism. By force. Among themselves they made no bones about it. Therefore it is no wonder that the republic took counter measures, including keeping track of this bunch of contentious and ineffectual revolutionaries.

There were scores of these people from all over the red spectrum. Some were salty old Abraham Lincoln Brigadiers, real bomb throwers. If the Spanish experience hadn't disillusioned them nothing could. Some were Beverly Hills Bolsheviks. For some reason they are now being beatified for their martyrdom. At most they lost some swell jobs. But Mexico wasn't Siberia, which is where their hero sent dissidents. Some were trots. Trotsky was murdered in Mexico by Stalinists, go figure.

For the purpose of keeping track of these diverse radicals it was necessary to invent a label, hence the ACGM. Basically they all knew each other and shared a loathing for constitutional democracy, but little else. They socialized but it was more of a newcomers' club than a red Rotary.

It fell to me to write an annual report on the ACGM, tough since it didn't exist. However I would cobble up a couple of hundred pages reviewing their identities and activities that year. There were a number of Mexican fringe associates, some of whom I understand were refused visas because of membership in the ACGM, which must have mystified them. Hey Mama, did you join the ACGM?

For some reason most were Jewish. It seemed to me that the Communist Party-USA (CPUSA) would have collapsed without the Jewish element (and without FBI informants, not necessarily mutually exclusive). I never understood this and would like to find a study on the subject. I once asked an American Jewish Progressive Femme (AJPF), (whoa this is addictive) and she said it was because AJPFs are compassionate.

But the times were changing, the old barricades and bombs fervor was fading. A lot of the old guard was red and dead.

I hated this work and managed to back down a lot of the blanket coverage of these barren and boring people singing their silly socialist songs and complaining about the help. It was amazing how much one could maneuver the policies of the monolithic Bureau by not bothering to ask.

Nevertheless it was still the Bureau. At every annual inspection we were required to specify the number of American Communists in Mexico in the past year. This worried me for awhile but finally I just added two or three to the number reported the previous year and everybody was happy.

The reason security work was so disagreeable to me was that unlike the criminal side there was rarely any satisfactory conclusion. Just keep the glaciers of paper moving. Even if you catch a spy they usually cut a deal.

Some guys are great at it. Parques was a wonderful man, wonderful agent, the senior man on the security side. Nothing ruffled him. He handled the top informants and mountains of paper with seeming ease. While I was writing the piddling little ACGM report he was writing the report on the Mexican Communist Party, an entirely different animal. The PCM was a large, powerful, sophisticated organization with thousands of members, actively supported by the Russians and Cubans, and quite capable of real revolution.

Parques would dictate for days straight, mostly off the top of his head, tying up the whole steno pool. The result would be a tome, hundreds of pages, all documented. Majestic. Had to impress even our "cousins" (The CIA). (Now I gotta kill you.)

A phenomenal performance, but like the Warren report, who would ever really review this material.

Someone did. Some beancounter in D.C. found some figure on page 597 where the peso amount had not been transposed to dollars, making a mistake of a million or so. So they censured Parques. Didn't seem to bother him much.

I often wonder what these old reds are thinking what with the collapse of the evil empire. I read somewhere that old Gus Hall was still a staunch Stalinist. Gus was no namby pamby parlor pinko.

The Federales

The border badmen movies make endless reference to the federales, but I never heard this usage in real life, what little I know of real life. Presumably they are referring to the Policía Judicial Federal, the Federal Judicial Police, often described as like the FBI. Like manzanas are like naranjas. Like the FBI it is under the Federal Attorney General, known as the Procurador General de la República, which always sounded like the republican general's pimp to me.

I loved going down to the Procuraduría, although not pronouncing it. The offices were scattered around great old double-arcaded courtyards in the historic precincts fronted by the Zócalo, the most ancient and architecturally honorable enclave on the continent.

The Chief of the Federal Judicial Police was usually career military, so often the administrative pool of the third world. Always changing, always cordial, often competent, often corrupt. The comandantes were career and in charge of actual investigations.

The Coronel in command of the Federal Police called me to get down to the Procuraduría. In Spanish, colonel is spelled coronel because Spanish is logical and phonetic, unlike some languages I could name. If I get too schoolmarmish, sit down and shut up before you get a ruler where it counts.

My interest was engaged well before I got to his office.

The old cobbled passageways along Correo Mayor were packed bumper to bosomly bumper with sparkling new American luxury cars. The chromed and finned cruisers of that era were extravagant exotica in Mexico where they were rare, prohibitively expensive and basically flagrantly illegal per se. Here there were dozens of them, drawing a huge, admiring crowd.

The Coronel was extremely pleased and with good cause. He and his men had broken up the biggest and most sophisticated car ring in my experience. Overnight. The Bureau would have been months on this thing but, contrary to what you might think, overnight was the Mexican way. Otherwise, pues, otherwise there would be influence and bribes and lawyers and quien sabe que.

The Coronel showed me a notebook, a sales catalogue actually, each page listing a late model, luxury car, registered in Texas.

The gang's contract thieves in Texas would spot a prime car in a parking garage. They could then arrange to copy the keys and note the home address on the registration. They would even case the home. Details were forwarded to their sales rep in Mexico, who went around with this notebook. You say you want a red Caddy convertible for half Blue Book? Pretty attractive deal. Cash only, delivery Friday.

Thieves could grab the car and deliver it in Mexico City the next day. Autos R' Us. The very flashiness did them in. Any one of these boats was a moving challenge to any officer. Grab one and back track to the rep and the catalogue.

It took days to process all these cars and weeks to track down all the data. There were a number of prosecutions on both sides.

The cars were all returned to Texas and we were able to add an astronomic recovery to Hoover's false figures for that year. I should have included street value, like the narcs. Actual street value on Correo Mayor was about three times sticker.

The Coronel was one of my particular favorites and I was deeply distressed to learn later that he was in jail in San Antonio on drug charges. There was a lot of that going around. I wonder what he was driving.

The Jefatura

The Mexico City Metropolitan Police was referred to as the Jefatura, the headquarters. The detective Division was called the Servicio Secreto, which the reader can easily translate unassisted. Everything was housed in a big ugly building due south of the Zócalo. The whole establishment was something of a miracle, policing a community larger and more disordered than New York on a fraction the budget.

It was, in effect, self-supporting. The Chief, the Jefe of the Jefatura, was again usually an Army officer, as was the chief of detectives, changed with each new president. The story goes that a new chief laid down the law the first day. No more payoffs. The comandantes looked at each other and filed by his desk with the usual hugs and handshakes. And envelopes. And that settled that. I don't condone corruption but the system left no alternative.

There were about a dozen comandantes, all tough, smart men, about the same number and fiber as the commanders I later worked with at Scotland Yard. Just a different jungle. A former comandante told me that the initiation into this fierce fraternity was to participate jointly in executing outlaws. Scandalous corruption finally ended the Secret Service and the senior commanders I worked with went to jail. To my regret. But there are jails and there are jails.

One of my favorite jefes was General Mendiolea, a little fireball in the shape of a bowling ball. Once Mendiolea sent word he had something to show me. Sí, mi general. He led me down a labyrinth of passageways to a huge holding area. The place was stuffed with raggedy, sullen, desperate looking men, seated on the floor with their hands bound behind them. There were scores of them and they were disconsolate, dance cards blank.

"Look at all these pinched goats" shrieked the general who had a shrill soprano surprising in a man who looked like a short sumo. "Comunistas, every pinche one of them." There had evidently been some sort of mass roundup of reds. This of course was not reported in the press, nor did it have anything to do with the Secret Service, which was itself unconstitutional anyway. But it was a great source of satisfaction to the General.

I was less pleased since he had just fingered me to every hard core commie in the Federal District. Obviously a gringo agent and the source of their torment. And all to be released, since there was no crime or jurisdiction. "Hi guys, hey, not my fault, I'm strictly a criminal agent, hate all this security stuff. Have a nice day."

Feelthy Fotos

The Secret Service usually called me when there was an American involved in some investigation and usually there turned out to be FBI interest. Often as not on making my daily rounds I went afoot, traffic and parking were horrendous. They called me that they had an American with a quantity of porno material. Interstate Transportation of Obscene Material (ITOM) was an FBI violation. But in paradoxically puritanical Mexico Playboy magazine was contraband. I would have to review this material.

There were hundreds of fotos, all male, and obsceneíssimo, by any community standards. Dozens of guys, including our friend, engaging in unimaginable stuff, including, to my astonishment, auto-fellatio.

They were packing a box of this stuff for me to take back to the Embassy. I would have to tediously catalogue and mark them and give them the special ITOM packaging designed to conceal them from the sensitive eyes of the clerical staff and of course achieving the exact opposite.

What if I got run over on the way back to the embassy? A distinct possibility in the D.F. The tabloids would scream "Foreign Officer Faggot Found with Feelthy Fotos". This wasn't a commercial operation and I doubted if any prosecutor would authorize.

Why not save time, money and aggro. I suggested they destroy the stuff and let the guy go with a warning. I gave him absolution. From what I had seen in the fotos he had suffered enough.

Mi Casa Es Su Casa

Everyone moving to Mexico dreams of a colonial home, patio, tiles, overwrought iron, beams, bougainvillea, huge carved doors. We moved a lot in Mexico City because of rising rents, and finally such a treasure fell our way. It was in the then distant colonia of Tecamachalco. It even had a trove of authentic colonial paintings of saints seeking eye drops.

One day some radical rag published a list purporting to be the names and addresses of all the CIA and FBI agents in Mexico, inviting interested readers to take appropriate action. They cobbled this out of the embassy phone book but it was pretty accurate. Lo, your servant's name led all the rest.

And that very night as we lay packed tight I was awakened by strange, subdued noises in the street below. I could see that numbers of 20ish kids were congregating silently right outside our door. Clearly a surreptitious rendezvous. There were few other houses. Cars kept drifting up, motors and lights killed.

What now. We had houseguests, including a newborn. We were outside the D.F. far from friends in the Jefatura. The Tecamachalco police could just about handle a stray goat. I had no firearms and wouldn't want to have. Well, colonial houses were built like fortresses for this very reason. Wait a bit.

Finally a keenly awaited van pulled up and out boiled a band of mustachioed ruffians, silver glinting from sombreros and sidearms. ZAPATAAA. It was a band. I see by your outfit that you are a mariachi. The band led the group around the corner and struck up the hauntingly beautiful and enigmatic "Las Mañanitas". It was a "gallo", the traditional predawn serenade. We have always loved mariachis and that tune.

Didn't have to awaken the house. The mariachi did that. Everyone loved a gallo, even at that hour. Prettiest music you ever heard.

Pepe le Moco

The Pepe case began, as many did, with a body found along the Carretera Vieja a Cuernavaca. Cuernavaca is a pretty resort city about an hour west of Mexico City. The Old Road twisted slowly through the mountains and was considered ideal for disposing of bodies, like a scenic New Jersey. Sometimes, seriously, sometimes a murderer would confess to such littering and the cops would sort through several before they came to the right stiff. And sometimes the Comandantes traveled this road.

Plus the road wound all over the place in and out of the Federal District and the State of Morelos a dozen times. Who would ever claim jurisdiction and Morelos had the worst police in the New World. One time a body was found along this road and identified as a revolutionary, a latter-day Zapata. The Chief of Police of Morelos complained to me bitterly about this carelessness. There was a perfectly good well not 100 meters away.

The murder was before my time but I had reviewed the many volumes and was familiar with the Pepe case. It was an extraordinary case, amazing that it was ever solved and that the perp was apprehended and sentenced.

The case was solved by the Comandante and Rafael, neither with a shred of jurisdiction. Rafael was our senior criminal agent, wonderful man, wonderful agent. There was a tendency to roll over incompetent malcontents. An experienced asset like Rafael was priceless. But he was an overachiever and made the mistake of qualifying in Portuguese. The post of Legal Attaché in Brazil came open and Rafael was selected, a merited advancement.

But Rafael had a large, complex family situation and such a move would have been a hardship, which he carefully explained in a letter to Mr. Hoover. By return mail he was busted a grade and given a disciplinary transfer to Miami, as far as possible from his home in Arizona.

He had done nothing wrong, in fact was the most effective agent around. I figured this transfer caused a round of musical chairs that cost the government hundreds of thousands of dollars and put all kinds of people in places where they were unhappy and thus ineffective and everyone got eczema.

"That ought to show them, Clyde" said Mr. H. contentedly as he turned out the lights. Nuthouse. Characteristic of the deliberate dumb mean-spiritedness that made the Bureau such a delight in those days.

This particular body was reported to the Jefatura. The Jefatura had some fine investigators and was not punctilious about jurisdiction or much of anything else, since they were probably an unconstitutional body themselves. Somehow they identified the body as Vito. Vito was an American so they notified Rafael at our Embassy.

Now that I think on it there was an enormous amount of information available very early on for just another bullet-ridden body on the Cuernavaca highway. And there was an enormous amount of money and influence in the wings. Probably coincidence.

It developed as a complex case with international ramifications, sex, drugs, Mafia, money, Cuban cartel, CIA, make a terrific miniseries.

Vito, like a lot of Vitos, enjoyed basking in bright lights and inferring mob connections. He had been seen around Mexico City with a curvy Cuban. And Pepe.

Pepe was the n'er-do-well nephew of a very wealthy New Yorker, heavy in the sugar biz, connections in Cuba. Sugar is a strange trade, lots of opportunity for hanky panky in the price, lots of margin for moving money.

Like a lot of rich kids Pepe liked to mess around with the mob. He came to Mexico and fell in with Vito. There was even a triangle, Vito, Pepe and La Cubana.

Next thing you know Vito's body is found at lookout point, his eyes now oblivious to the beauty about. It was established that Pepe had left Mexico but returned with a false identity and the firearms and was with Vito on his last night. It was ironclad. I think there was even an eyeball.

Somehow Pepe managed to get himself identified, apprehended, prosecuted and sentenced, in spite of enormous efforts by his family. No one said he was a mastermind. He had been in jail a good many years now and was no doubt a better man.

But the family was still frantic to get him out, and must have listened to dozens of scenarios.

They made a movie of the escape. The Bronson character was a scruffy, scofflaw bush pilot out of Texas, well known to Customs. He hired some poor kid chopper pilot from 'Nam and rented a wreck of a helicopter. They stashed fuel in dumps along the way and staged the chopper down. A rendezvous was set and the kid picked up Pepe and some pal from the prison yard. They hadn't factored the extra weight or the altitude but the ailing whirlybird finally lifted off and they flew back to Texas after abandoning the chopper.

It was a gawdawful plan but it worked. I called Texas but I don't think there was much activity. There was no computer then and everyone was watching the Canadian border. Allez allez ox in free.

The Judicial Police of the Federal District.

La Policía Judicial del Distrito Federal (PJDF), easily translated by our now adept reader, prided itself on being the primary constitutional investigative force for Mexico City. That it was tiny and insignificant compared to the hated Jefatura was not material.

The Chief of the PJDF for much of this time was Melchor Cardenas, a wonderful, old-time, overweight, policía-político with another of those great names. Don Melchor had a deep booming voice and a fine line of toro-taffy. He was host once at a huge police picnic. Several of us from the Embassy were guests of honor. Some fool Comandante in his cups got up on his folding chair and got way out of line with references to the colossus of the North and pobre de Mexico, so near the U.S. and so far from God.

Don Melchor, bless his big heart, jumped up and took command with his big, sonorous voice. His theme was that he had worked with the norteamericanos all his life and generally considered them to be responsible neighbors. He invited anyone who didn't agree to imagine the situation if it were Russia looming across the Río Bravo. Bravo indeed don Melchor!

So I really liked don Melchor. Besides he gave great hugs.

Then along came Jesse James.

Jesse James Roberts

Jesse James Roberts, another great name. I think the name was the problem. Jesse was a great big huge good old boy from Arkansas who had fallen into the habit of robbing banks. His folks should have named him Grover Cleveland Roberts. He wasn't a very good bank robber. He was big as a barn door and easily identified. Next thing you know he is on the Top Ten Fugitive list. That name again.

Jess came to Mexico with a duffel bag full of cash withdrawn from reluctant banks and an urge to enjoy himself. Vino y violines. (c'mon, it's easy, sound it out). He was moving around a lot and we could never quite catch up with him although we had turned out the whole office, including clerks and contract investigators. How hard can it be, he is two meters tall carrying duffel, a bimbo on each arm.

I later learned that he was camped for awhile in a VW bus with two broads on the beach on the old dirt road between Acapulco and Zihuatanejo and we had driven right by his little idyll.

Then he popped up in the capital again and damned if he wasn't doing the regular Kodak-carrying tourist bit. He had a covey of locals as guides and they loved to see him dip into that duffel.

This was getting annoying. I was working around the clock coordinating the investigation. Sunday morning one of the contract investigators called. He had located Jesse at the Lagunilla, the local flea market. Call out the cavalry.

We were strictly enjoined from making any apprehensions ourselves. They were supposed to be coordinated through Gobernación, the omnipotent interior department.

We had alerted Gobernación but it was Sunday morning. They had no cars, no radio, no duty officer, nothing. So I frantically started calling around to the other agencies with some claim to manpower and jurisdiction. Nada.

Finally I got hold of Comandante Chaley at the PJDF, a fantastic stroke of luck. Chaley had plenty of cojones, capability and constitutionality. Chaley got clearance from don Melchor and got on his horse. Within the hour don Melchor called. Chaley and his squad had found Jesse in the Lagunilla as advertised and even as we spoke was en route to PJDF HQ.

Maybe a big game hunter who has spent thousands of dollars and hours and finally bags a trophy feels similar excitement. Bursting with elation I sped to PJDF HQ to the fat, welcoming arms of don Melchor. We embraced and thumped each other and awaited the arrival of Comandante Chaley and the quarry. And waited and waited. The Lagunilla was as close to the PJF HQ as the Embassy. The effusiveness was evaporating.

Finally after several tense hours Chaley showed up with Jesse and the famous duffel bag of cash. Chaley explained that they had taken Jesse by his digs to pick up his effects. The duffel was stashed in don Melchor's safe and subsequently delivered with Jesse to Gobernación for processing and deportation.

When things were sorted out I returned to the office to scenes of great jubilation. Not every day a Top Ten was run down. More hugs from the Legal Attaché, at that time a very decent gentleman, if not nearly so cuddly as don Melchor.

Two problems developed very shortly.

Don Melchor and Chaley were both very experienced and sophisticated officers. I stressed to them and they knew perfectly well that there should be no publicity. But the press was generous and the PJDF was a sieve. Soon the tabloids were full of the story. "Valiant Mexican Police Capture Famous Giant Gringo Bandido Jesse James". Etc. That name again.

The Secretary of Gobernación, a heartbeat from the presidency, was not pleased. Cooperative arrangements were on the basis of no publicity.

The other problem was the loot. We knew that Jesse had about $70,000 in the duffel. We well knew he was spending freely in Mexico. When he and the duffel got to the border an inventory produced about $30,000. Jesse claimed there was about $60,000 when he was arrested. This was embarrassing for all. It appeared very much like someone somewhere along the way had decided on a fifty-fifty split, probably considered it a generous compromise under the circumstances.

The Secretary of Government, the number 2 man in Mexico and the next president, called in the Legal Attaché and your very humble servant for a royal butt roast.

I was officially commended and officially censured for the same case.

When in the fullness of time the Secretary became El Señor Presidente he achieved fame as the greatest thief in Mexican history. Jesse James was a piker.

Fuchi Mugre

Oh Lord, not another Spanish lesson.

No, another kidnapping case. These are always stressful cases, especially in a case like this where the fate of the victim was not known. In this case the pressure was cranked up a notch by the presence of Assistant Director Marco Fieltro who had taken personal charge of the case on scene in Los Angeles. This was rare and usually a disaster since few of the ADs had any field experience or competence.

But Fieltro, who became in effect the operating chief of the FBI before the inevitable falling out with Hoover, was an exception. He had a lot of intelligence and experience. He personally had inspected us once and did a bang up job, also rare for an AD. He even punctiliously paid all his tabs, unheard of in the Hoover hierarchy.

The victim was a girl missing under suspicious circumstances from the family home in Los Angeles. We all wanted to find the girl, find the kidnaper, and do a good job for Fieltro.

The prime suspect was in Mexico City. He was primíssimo. He was a black who had come from Africa to study. He had lived with the victim's family before disappearing into the night. He was known to be a heavy user of drugs and a general no good, bongo-playing bum.

For a case like this we mobilized the whole office and all the contract players. The resources were limited but we had no package as yet to discuss with the authorities. And it was important not to alert the suspect. Even so it was almost frightening to me how much information can be developed discreetly in a short time by competent, motivated investigators.

We soon located him and had him covered like a blanket. It was clear that he did not have the girl with him.

The next step was to get him back to California. He had not been charged with kidnaping but there were other charges pending against him. It was easy to establish he was illegally in Mexico, he was a walking immigration violation. Gobernación was more than happy to cooperate in his deportation, he was highly undesirable. Kidnaping was rare in those days and Mexican officialdom regarded it with horror.

As part of the package Fieltro demanded repeatedly that all the suspect's possessions must accompany him to the border when he was deported. This could be priceless evidentiary and lead material. I stressed the importance of this with the Mexican officials and they were in accord.

It was days of working around the clock but everything went like clockwork. Immigration agents went to his flat early and had no problem. They stuffed the subject and his effects in the subject's old car, took him to HQ for processing and were on their way in hours. The whole package was delivered to our authorities waiting at the border the same night.

I was extremely pleased, this had been a difficult and delicate operation.

The Mexican government immigration agents were well known to me. I knew all the agents and had a lot of respect for them and their agency. Fine, experienced, reliable men, never a hint of payoffs or brutality, a delight to work with. I had worked with this particular pair many times.

On their return from the border I met with them to thank and congratulate them and to make sure that all the subject's effects had gone with him to the border.

They assured me that nothing was left in the apartment but "mugre", and that is what I reported to Mr. Fieltro.

Now "mugre" is one of my favorite words. It means filth, grime, only worse. Like another of my favorites, "fuchi" (disgusting), it even sounds like what it represents. They defy exact translation, you have to make a face when you say them. In this case we knew the guy lived like a pig and the word conveyed as no other, a filthy, filthy flat.

Later with the same sort of part-time punctilio that has always plagued me I went to the flat and gained entry. I found to my horror that it was stuffed floor to ceiling with junk, tons of it, one could not even move about. Heaven knows where he had collected all this crap, especially in Mexico where thousands lived by free-lance scavenging. Mountains of useless junk, would have filled a dumpster.

My immigration agents had obviously looked at all this stuff and looked at each other and decided this moldy refuse was valueless. Mugre.

Murphy's law had kicked in. If I reported this now all hell would break loose. Fieltro would demand it be seized and forwarded. It would take weeks to review and process and catalogue all this rubbish. In addition I had no way to claim it, I wasn't there legally and the guy wasn't even American. It could never be used as evidence and might taint what we had. I quietly closed the door and stole away.

It looked like mugre to me. Fuchi too.

It shortly developed that our suspect, although a lawbreaker and screwup, had nothing to do with the kidnapping. And I returned to sleeping nights. Now that I think back the landlady probably would have been happy to have someone take out all that trash. Oh well.

The Mad Doctor

The mad doctor had invented the ultimate invisible ink.

He actually was a doctor, some sort of displaced mittel European, who had found refuge in Mexico where he prospered in the movie popcorn business. And he wasn't mad, quite a nice old gentleman, in fact. But he was obsessed with this ink he invented.

Found out later that he used to hang out at the American Legion club annoying the regular bores with tales of this wonderful stuff. Probably to shut him up someone suggested he write Washington.

Somehow this arrived on the desk of Assistant Director Mulligan. Mulligan was a brilliant man and a riveting speaker but a world class eccentric himself. He was totally dedicated to the security field, which the reader knows by now suggests a lack of common sense. He was in charge of all that spook stuff and anxious to steal a march on our cousins, the CIA. My boss was a Mulligan protégé.

The doc had made all kinds of claims for his stuff. Not only was it invisible, it was also odorless, colorless, undetectable, self-incinerating, non-incriminating, non-discriminating and cured baldness.

Mulligan got on the horn with his pet and it was decided to check this out. I got the ticket. Hey, I'm criminal, I could see no FBI utility for the finest invisible ink imaginable.

The doc's bonafides check out fine. He had a scientific background and was a respected member of the community. An appointment was made for the doc to come in and demonstrate.

The doc was in his glory. He had spent years polishing this spiel and it would have gone over great at the County Fair. He had dozens of felt-tip pens loaded with different blends of his goop. He had swatches of cloth and paper and smoke and mirrors he taped to the walls, now you see it, now you don't.

The whole production took about 90 minutes from a busy day and could not be forestalled. If he were interrupted he would just start all over again. This was his life and nothing short of decapitation would stop him.

And the stuff worked a treat, did all kinds of cute tricks, appeared, disappeared, reappeared, changed colors, decorated Easter eggs, changed gothic to pica, polarized, whatever he claimed it would do.

Naturally he wasn't going to give away this priceless formula but because of his warm feelings he would make this magic available. To the USA. All he asked in return was airfare and expenses to Washington for a demonstration.

This was relayed by my jefe to Mulligan and there were a number of calls and consultations and by golly they authorized the trip. Which means that Hoover was consulted since he approved every expenditure over $50. Really.

Next thing you know the doc is on a flight to D.C. where he is met and escorted to the JEH building where an interagency group of tech specialists had been assembled. Mulligan of course had sponsored this show. Teach them CIA snots a thing or two.

I can see the whole production. I know from bitter experience that nothing can deter the mad doc once his gearbox is engaged.

All these busy experts rolling their eyes and watching the time. Finally the doc finishes, ta da, and modestly steps aside.

Some smartass CIA tec pulls out a black light and all this stuff fluoresces like Times Square.

Mulligan is furious. He had sponsored this project and now he looks like a fool. Why hadn't we checked this out!

Well I had asked the doc if the stuff responded to black light and he claimed it would not respond to black, ultra, infra, or stop lights nor to gamma, beta, X or Billy rays. I had no way to test his claim.

By now I imagine there is a black light gathering dust in every equipment vault in every office.

Myself, I just never found that much use for special invisible inks. Lemon juice served well in the Boy Scouts. Anyway I usually use a ballpoint pen. Handy for turning the dial of the Orphan Annie decoder ring.

Comandante Peaches

As in San Juan the airport in Mexico City was part of my beat. I was in regular contact with the American carriers and the many officials at the airport, immigration, customs, security, etc., but the main contact was the Judicial Police, headed for many years by Comandante Peaches. The Comandante was like a medieval baron with his own fiefdom. Peaches was a bit crude but bright and energetic. A lot of these officers skipped charm school.

We got a call that there was a skyjacking in progress on an American flight originating at Mexico City. This was one of the first skyjackings. I raced to the airport. Jorge Afilado, the other criminal agent, couldn't go because lunchtime was approaching. He never missed lunch.

The Judicial Police had a suite of offices hidden away in the upper, inner passageways. It was a small detail mainly concerned with narcotics. All too often the office was vacant. Now it was jammed. Peaches and a dozen of his best men. They were only too aware of the skyjacking, having been advised by the American who was stationmaster for the airlines. These stationmasters were demi-gods in those days and places.

Some nut with a gun had taken over a flight, which was even then circling Monterrey, far to the north. It was imperative to identify the nut so as to help in dealing with him. It was an international flight, there should be plenty of data available on the passengers.

Unfortunately in an ill-conceived gesture to enlist aid the manager had authorized lunch for the police detail. So they were in the middle of lunch. Waiter after waiter was arriving with course after course on covered trays, a parade that continued through the long afternoon.

A traditional lunch in Mexico took hours.

I was frantic to access the records and identify the jacker. A lot of these records were sacrosanct, Mexicans could be remarkably officious. The ideal vehicle for obtaining this data was a Federal Judicial Policeman. Here was a room full of them.

Peaches would assign an agent to work with me and we would start the laborious review process. But after awhile he took his place back in the food chain. Then I would literally drag another agent away from the trough only to have him disappear. Awful afternoon.

But bit by bit we were able to come up with information that proved useful to the people who were dealing with the subject. The plane was now on the ground in Monterrey. Our man in Monterrey was an Afilado clone who had to be shown how to use the pay phone to telephone the wifey he might be late for dinner.

Finally they got custody of the subject and it was all over except for hours and hours of more paper work.

Afilado was always punctilious about calling his wife every afternoon. Not to say he would be late, he was never late. To find our what was for dinner.

Peaches made the most of his fiefdom. He later achieved fame as the head of the Mexico City Police and reputed pimp and bagman for the president. But he later went to jail. His opulent mansion on the Old Road to Cuernavaca is now the government museum of corruption. Seriously.

Al Portador

Like many Italians, Al tended to talk out of the side of his mouth and hint he was heavy with the mob. No, I'm kidding. That was Joe Tampoco. Seriously "Al Portador" means "to the bearer", like bearer bonds. Everything sounds better in Spanish, like for instance any Christian name. What did you say your name was honey?

Bearer bonds, payable to any person who presents them, according to my Black's Law Dictionary. Same like cash, according to jailhouse lore. We used to get inquiries on this stuff all the time. Beautiful paper, engraved and embossed and beribboned. But the source and price clearly showed hanky panky. Sometimes informants would furnish the numbers and the brokerage and we still couldn't trace them. Apparently there was a lot of sloppy warehousing on Wall Street.

Same like cash, but trot it around to the bank where your brother-in-law knows the manager and try to walk out with cash. Folks who deal in cash seem reluctant to part with it.

Manny, Moto and Jack were three unlikely stock swindlers. Two suitable, inscrutable, indisputable Orientals and a surfer. Actually fairly decent men and I don't know how they got caught up in this caper that ruined their lives.

The stooges presented themselves at the International Department on the mezzanine of the new Banco Internacional, on Paseo de la Reforma, Mexico, D.F., Mexico. They had a picnic basket full of this pretty paper, bearer bonds. The bank and its staff were new, young and aggressive. But not stupid. They wouldn't trade cash for this paper but they agreed to forward it through channels for collection.

The trio called back frequently to check on the deal. The bank forwarded the paper and, as we had found so often, there was no record of it being stolen. Eventually it was traced to the inventory of a major brokerage that didn't know it was missing. Meanwhile somehow it was cleared and the trio was so advised.

They reappeared at the bank and no one there will ever forget the scene. There were only a dozen employees of the

International Department and they were scurrying all over the skyscraper trying to scrape up all this cash in dollars, $40 or $50,000.

The trio couldn't be bothered to tally the total, they were stuffing bills into their suits and shirts and literally into their hats. They gleefully took their departure down the escalator, everybody waving in a grand demonstration of international amity.

It would appear that they had found a patsy bank.

About a month later the trio flew back to Mexico with another basket of bonds for their new friends at the Banco Internacional. They might have noticed less warmth in the greeting. The bonds had finally been traced. Lawsuits are still pending.

This time descending the escalator from the mezzanine they were escorted by agents from the excellent Office of Special Investigations of the Banco de México, the national bank.

They denied everything, denied knowledge of the bonds, denied they had even been in the bank, denied they were oriental. They were turned over to the judicial authorities and finally sentenced to serious time.

I visited with them from time to time in the Black Palace of Lecumberri, sometimes at their request, sometimes not. I felt very sorry for them. The Asians were decent, family men whose businesses had fallen on hard times. Thinking back I would suspect gambling losses. The disgrace was ruinous to them and their families and I doubt they profited much.

Jack was an engaging young Murph the Surf type and became a pet at the prison. He soon spoke street Spanish and even the mythic prison dialect "caló", and embassy and prison officers used him to translate.

Naturally both governments wanted to know the source of these bonds. Nobody thought the stooges had stolen them. I couldn't offer them any kind of a deal but they obviously thought I could, thought I could spring them. But they never said a word, not a peep.

Hoover may not have believed in the Mafia but the stooges sure did.

The Grungy Genius

Pepito Perdido, Jr. came to the American Embassy in Mexico to report that his father, Pepe Sr., had traveled to the U.S. and now was missing, feared kidnaped. We got missing reports all the time and the FBI could do little. Kidnaping was very serious indeed. If anyone was a candidate for going missing it was Pepe Perdido. The family acknowledged that he owed everybody in three states. I didn't take this very seriously.

Then the demand notes started appearing.

They were very strange demand notes. They were undoubtedly written in Pepe's handwriting and sent recently from the Washington area, providing ample federal jurisdiction. The notes were Xeroxes, not originals. They were full of instructions about the redeployment of the investment of Gaylord Grunge, which both Pepe and the family knew was not possible. And they contained no actual throat-cutting threat. This was beginning to smell menacing and federal indeed.

The family knew Grunge perfectly well and suspected him from the beginning.

Grunge was a young American who had come to Mexico with a million dollars to invest, a well-documented million in cash. He had deposited this fortune with the international department of a major bank and was basically home free. Comparatively high, safe and tax-free income forever. (Actually in retrospect it might have all fallen to the devaluations.)

Boy he sure didn't look or act like a millionaire. He was a walking fashion disaster, filthy, unkempt, unwashed clothes, uncut hair, he made Arafat look like Astaire. He made up for his sloppy appearance with a vile attitude.

He lived out of the back of an old pickup with a camper bed parked in a campground south of the city. He was dirty and rude and smelly and people hated to be around him.

But everyone I talked to, and I talked to scores over the years, commented on his intelligence. It is very hard to quantify IQ socially but he was sure impressing these people. He was bright alright, arguably the smartest criminal of the century. A PhD in math from Harvard for starters.

Then he fell afoul of Pepe Perdido. Although bust, Pepe had a swank storefront on Paseo de la Reforma. Pepe was some package. A born con man he had been involved in land fraud in the border city of Ciudad Juárez, State of Chihuahua, the bustling industrial center of Monterrey, State of Nuevo León, and the resort area of Acapulco, State of Guerrero. All these cities figure prominently in the annals of land fraud and Pepe was subject to arrest in all three states.

But he wasn't a bad guy. He was in his fifties, well dressed, very well spoken in both languages,. Affable and cultured and charming. He was also a Bible-thumping evangélico, an important and apparently authentic part of his persona. He used this façade to fleece flocks on both sides.

A good tin man truly believes in aluminum siding.

He must have had good qualities because he had a wonderful family who adored him and they were desperately worried.

Somehow, and this is difficult to believe but well documented, Grunge wandered into Pepe's lair and fell for his song and dance. He liquidated the account in the bank and transferred the assets to Pepe's brokerage. Presumably he hoped to multiply his return.

The uncouth Grunge was welcomed into the bosom of the cultured Perdidos, but the honeymoon was soon over. Grunge must shortly have discovered the investment was shaky and wanted out. But liquidity was not a feature of a Perdido promotion. Things were getting tense and ugly. Grunge demanded his money but Pepe explained that it was frozen in the land scheme in Acapulco.

About this time Pepe got some promising calls from the D.C. area. The caller spoke fluent evangelical and claimed to represent a flock with spare funds. They wanted Pepe to fly up and discuss investments in Mexico. Like inviting a coyote to discuss chicken. The family was dubious but Pepe insisted on making the trip. He had to. The till was nil. He was to be met at Dulles International Airport by the erstwhile lambs. He was never seen again.

Dulles has several interesting aspects. It is a million miles from anywhere and it is on a federal reservation.

Pepe always called his dear family daily. Now no calls. Instead these strange letters.

The family believed, quite rightly, that Grunge had lured Pepe to Dulles, kidnaped him, and forced him to write these letters. Soon, sadly, the letters stopped. But cables were flying.

From practically the first cable we learned that we were not dealing with Gaylord Grunge at all.

My opening cable was titled "UNSUB" (Unknown Subject) (UNSUB flags that a certain identity has not been established) "aka" (also known as) Gaylord Grunge. A sleepy file clerk thumbing through indices at HQ found there was already an UNSUB aka Gaylord Grunge case. An espionage case. Espionage got nearly as much priority as kidnaping.

In his many travels Grunge had transited the San Antonio airport. This was the skyjack era and he fit the profile like King Kong's condom. He looked like a walking threat to civilization and sanitation and acted strange, the only way he knew how to act. Some alert marshal pulled him out of line to check his bona fides and he nervously produced not one but two passports.

This information was relayed to the FBI. Very suspicious. It was soon established that Gaylord Grunge was a child buried in the historic El Paso cemetery after a tragic death at the age of one. Cruising a graveyard for such an identity was standard spy skullduggery.

The other passport was in the name Rube Harvard.

The marshal may only now be learning that through the sort of officiousness that I deplore, she solved a major case and saved the government a mountain of money. Some agents seemed to patronize the U.S. marshals. Not me, they helped me a lot on several big cases. But they also pulled me out of line at airports twice, sanctimonious sons of she-camels.

Rube Harvard was from some dirt poor southern trash type background but had somehow scrambled his way to a doctorate in higher math from Harvard. He then proceeded to make his million by designing a computer program and selling it to some conglomerate. They complained later that the program was tainted but declined to go to court. Barely thirty and home free.

He had a complex master plan, the money, false identities, safe houses and drop boxes. He planned meticulously and executed atrociously. This was the Rube signature, thank heaven. Make a million and then mismanage it. Cook up a false passport and then fumble it away. Xerox the ransom letters to confound the lab and then leave a latent print on the Xerox.

The master swindler out-foxed by the amiable evangelist. He must have been furious. So he concocted another plot.

The lure of the gospel group with excess funds was surefire. It was apparent that he had enticed Pepe up to Virginia and then forced him to write these letters. And then no more letters. It seemed fairly certain there had been a kidnaping probably followed by murder, with all sorts of international ramifications and complications.

A major case by any standards. But it never got major case attention. All the work was done by myself and a fine agent in Virginia and our dance cards were already overflowing. I wept when I heard some defense counsel refer to the mighty resources of the government. There were endless Mexican aspects and a Mexican murdered in the U.S. was a violation of Mexican law. I made an unprecedented appeal to the Mexican Attorney General, nada. Foreigners might imagine Mexican officialdom to be indolent. Nothing could be further from the truth. They just were not interested in this case. Pepe had burned his bridges.

The excellent Agent in Virginia had gotten a warrant for Harvard aka Grunge for kidnaping but we expected plenty of trouble finding and prosecuting him. We knew he had help and was moving constantly. Living out of the truck made him harder to trace but his bad karma pursued him.

He was overnighting in some campground in S. Squalor, Oklahoma. As usual he pissed off everyone in sight and hearing and drove off leaving a mess. A nosy neighbor had noticed him surreptitiously disposing of some documents, so she dug them up and trotted them down to the nearest FBI office.

I have been on duty many times when such packages have been presented by the helpful citizenry. SOP was thank you ma'am and trash can. But some punctilious duty agent reviewed this stuff and it seemed to outline clandestine procedures. More spy stuff. And it turned out to be Rube's network, saving us all kinds of time.

It developed that Doctor Rube Harvard, exact same particulars, was teaching math at a prep school in Maryland. An apprehension party was soon organized and Dr. Harvard was soon in the D.C. cooler, where he had an unfortunate romantic interlude with a large roomie.

Early and loudly he was protesting that he wasn't Harvard after all. He claimed he was Calvin Cootie. Calvin was one of life's losers and an accomplice to Harvard. Rube had lent him the credentials to get this job. It is staggering to imagine Calvin pumping Pythagoras into preppies.

Calvin was soon begging to reveal the whole sorry saga.

At Rube's instigation Calvin had made the telephone calls to Pepe, claiming to represent the Bethesda Bible group. Pepe knew this bait would fish and it did.

Calvin helped Rube form a reception committee for Pepe when he flew into Dulles. Dulles, an airport on a government reservation near D.C. during the skyjack era, seems a poor choice for a kidnap venue but it worked.

Pepe was driven off in Rube's camper. The family started getting the letters. The next few days can't have been pleasant. Both Rube and Pepe must have known there was only one ending to this sorry scenario. Rube showed Calvin a sack of teeth.

I assume Pepe is slumbering in Chesapeake Bay. I hope his undoubtedly sincere beliefs were a comfort.

Because the Dulles complex is in the rolling countryside of Virginia the matter was scheduled to go to trial in federal court in enchanting Virginia. The government has assembled witnesses from all over the world. The lawyers were future stars of the D.C. bar.

The day of the trial Rube waltzed in and copped a plea. After the usual litany of judicial safeguards (which safeguard only the judge) the plea was accepted. The bargain was probably a wise accommodation. It would have been a long, costly, complex trial. The fine Perdido family seemed to realize this was the best of a bad situation. They were Americanophiles anyway and gringo justice had moved montañas.

There was a very subdued celebration and everyone went home. Papa Pepe was not going home but neither was Rube.

At the requisite semi-celebratory dinner the official translator asked if wasn't true that living in a foreign country affected one's thoughts and speech. I said I dint thin so.

Post Script

Years later in London I participated in a huge international conference on kidnaping sponsored by Scotland Yard. This terrible crime was increasing on the continent and as the supposed pre-eminent specialists the FBI was requested to take a leading role.

The Bureau had sent a very sharp young supervisor from the kidnap section to make a presentation. As a prop he had brought with him a huge roll of paper, a drum a foot wide, which was unscrolled all around the huge auditorium. The latest thing, a new take on graphing.

This was on the Grunge case. My case.

Several high-octane specialists had spent weeks cobbling up this vast torah of time study. Actually not a bad idea. This was a very complex case, much more so than might appear from this modest narrative. All the pertinent events were charted and correlated. One could go to any place on the chart and document the pertinent activities at that time.

It was a good idea and would have been of benefit to the prosecutors and especially to the jury. And some of that time and effort would have helped the investigation.

But it finally turned out to be of great aid to me since it helped me to make my point and I had staggered to the podium unencumbered with any point at all. Paper management is paramount in major cases but useless without the early dedication of sufficient resources.

I think that is what I said.

Show Me Your Shard

Another late night call from the Jefatura. Some gringo in a big Cadillac had gone tearing through the charming cobbled streets that characterize the lovely old San Angel section of the city and had smashed into a car carrying a Mexican family, all of whom were seriously injured. The gringo, who had no documentation for himself or the car, was in custody.

ITSMV, Interstate Transportation of Stolen Motor Vehicles, the Dyer Act. The bureau caught a lot of flack for chasing these cheesy cases as part of Hoover's relentless quest for meaningless statistics. Such cases were not popular with street agents but often provided a lever to larger things.

One reason they were not popular was that processing a recovered vehicle could be drudgery. Processing them all properly would exhaust all the resources and storage capability. Still, one never knew. Once I processed a stolen pickup found in the desert in California. Under the seat I found a crumpled receipt which I duly forwarded to Phoenix. Only years later did I learn it was key to solving a murder there.

The National Automobile Theft Bureau, sponsored by the insurance companies, was a big help in such cases, their agents were far more expert in the arcane art of processing stolen vehicles. Pineapple Corner was the NATB man in Mexico and he was a real bulldog. For that very reason the police never called him. He was forever reporting some high official driving around in a car stolen in the U.S., embarrassing for all. Hell, the official didn't know the car was stolen any more than Hoover knew hotels charged for rooms. Actually Hoover motored many a mile in seized vehicles.

Clearly these resources must be used with restraint. However, since this was an UNSUB whose description matched a current Top Ten Fugitive, I arranged for Pineapple to give the Caddy a real shakedown. He found a good latent fingerprint, which he duly lifted and preserved. Unfortunately he chose to transfer it to a bit of broken glass, not textbook. Ni modo. I forwarded the fragile artifact to Washington and voilá, a positive identification.

The subject was not Top Ten but was a hood from Chicago with a rep and a rap. The Mexicans were happy to deport him and the feds in Chicago were happy to prosecute him for ITSMV. Precious little help to the Mexican family but a plus for society.

The subject demanded a trial and Pineapple and I went to Chicago as witnesses. Somehow the shattered shard survived and Pineapple was a great witness. To the great satisfaction of all the subject was convicted and sentenced. Clang, Clang Clank went the clink door.

It didn't seem to matter that he wasn't really guilty of ITSMV. The car wasn't technically stolen. The Caddy belonged to some putz who gave it to his son. Like many in Chi the son liked to mix with the mob and lent the car to the subject, who destroyed it in Mexico. The son naturally reported it stolen.

Justice was served but it was disturbing. Apparently everyone in the courtroom but your humble servant and Pineapple knew the true story. There is a lot of hypocrisy in our system.

At least it was safety glass. Any other glass would not have survived and neither would the case.

Philip Agee

For the 1968 Olympics in Mexico the Embassy very wisely established the office of Olympic Attaché. It made tremendous sense to have a central coordinating office under professional direction. Everyone in the Embassy did Olympic-related work and there were millions of details.

It wasn't unusual for the CIA to put their people in an Embassy under State Department cover. I knew and worked with a number of such people and never had any problem. As far as I was concerned CIA had the superior mandate, the defense of the realm. They were usually competent and professional in these positions, a point of pride. I had no idea then how sloppy CIA was in the selection and supervision of such people.

Philip Agee was named Olympic Attaché. He seemed pleasant and personable but he was absolutely hopeless. He never returned calls or responded to messages, he was never in his office. There were torrents of tasks to coordinate, hosting the hundreds of athletes, the thousands of visitors, tickets, security, times, reservations. Nada. No Felipe.

Fortunately State had also recruited an Assistant Olympics Attaché, David Carrasco. David was a tall young Latino coach from the borderlands, far removed from the whitebread, white shoe Agee. David was a wonder, always available, always agreeable, always responsive, competent, decisive, worked day and night and thoroughly charmed everyone.

The Mexicans were moving mountains to organize this event properly and proudly, quite aware of the doubts about their capabilities and of the leftist efforts to sabotage the effort. Everyone in the Embassy was equally determined for success. All but Agee.

Agee had another agenda. He didn't even want western democracy to succeed, let alone the Olympics.

Olympic Attaché was an enormously prestigious position and State had let CIA put their man in this post. A man who was already working for the communists. He was never in the office because he was out wining and dining CIA targets, which he then turned over to the Soviets, completely out of the control of State and obviously the CIA.

Shortly thereafter Agee went on to infamy defecting to the Soviets and exposing every CIA contact he knew or imagined, destroying lives, reputations, relations, projects.

Our government spends billions on vetting procedures to avoid such treason knowing the USSR was actively recruiting. The irony is that Agee, like the fatuous FBI fool Miller, the brilliant Brit Kim Philby and now Ames were all actively recruited by their agencies for elitist reasons and all had problems getting entry to the Soviets.

Meanwhile superb, proven candidates like David Carrasco, who wanted a place at either agency, are passed over. David went back to El Paso where he achieved mythic status in community work before meeting a tragic end.

We should have been recruiting the Carrascos. There should be an Olympic medal for David Carrasco.

Sam the Man

Sam Giancana was the head of the Chicago syndicate and the most notorious crime figure of his era. The last ten years of his life were lived in Mexico under the protection of some powerful patron and the bemused eye of your humble servant.

Perhaps no Mafia don ever lived so well. He had luxurious estates in Cuernavaca, the land of eternal Spring an hour from Mexico City, and a penthouse apartment in the capital. He had ample and attentive help, a housekeeper, maids, a cook, gardeners, even a butler. He played his beloved golf regularly, in Cuernavaca and at the exclusive Churrubusco Club in Mexico City.

His mistresses, including the MacGuire sister and the lady he shared with JFK, flew in regularly. He had a circle of card-playing cronies. Best of all he had some kind of big fix with the Mexican government, and maybe with the U.S. government. He could even travel extensively and safely, sending friends cheery postcards from Madrid and Beirut. He had it made.

Still one must wonder if any thinking Mafioso ever sleeps really well. I used to think I might have caused him some sleepless nights. Probably not. But he knew I was out there pecking away at his little paradise.

When this case was first assigned to me my heart sank. It was exciting to be investigating such a fabled figure. It was also obvious that he had powerful clout in Mexico. I assumed I was going to be ordered to get him out. The same thing happened years later when the Robert Vesco case was assigned to me. I expected that the Bureau and the Department of Justice would be demanding coverage far beyond my poor powers. Not so, nothing, nada. Never got any positive direction or instruction at all in either case. A relief, but frightening.

On a review of the Sam file I found to my surprise that there was no fugitive warrant or prosecutive process. In ten years of holding this ticket I never got a meaningful lead or instruction from the Department, FBH HQ or Chicago, the Office of Origin.

I had just come from Tampa where there were a dozen men full time on the old numbers runner Trafficante.

I was told several times that Hoover was personally interested in the Giancana case, scary in itself. He never said anything to me. He told me on two occasions that Merle Oberon had a social disease but that didn't strike me as interesting or relevant. I admired her work as an actress but considered congress unlikely. Hooverlandia.

Actually it turned out to be a very comfortable case, a perfect case actually. Interesting, challenging, perplexing, occasionally rewarding, and no pressure whatsoever. I could chip away at it in my spare time and send out a letter every month or two on what I had developed, quite a lot over the years, and even more that I didn't bother to report. Never any incoming. Spooky.

Speaking of spooky I realized early on that CIA was fudging on Sam. I would trot Sam by them every year and every year their name check chick would disappear for a long, long time and then come back to say they had nothing. If they had nothing on a major Mafioso on their turf they should give up the intelligence dodge or invent a better story.

Still I realized that they often played such games and that it was necessary. I chased some wild bandido fugitive all over Latin America for years and later found out he was reporting to Customs every month.

Now there is ample public source material to document that CIA had approached Sam about eliminating Castro. No self-respecting government should ever gang up with the goons. Lucky Luciano should have resolved that. (On the other hand surely the allies would have considered anything to off Hitler.)

It could pretty much be assumed that Sam was in Mexico and had a carefully crafted cover. If Chicago had bothered to advise that Sam was a demon golfer I could have located him in a week and maybe had some fun. As it was, ironically, I located him through Richard Scalzetti Cain, Sam's factotum. Cain, who has his own richly deserved chapter, was a bent Chicago cop with contacts in Mexico. Part of his job was Sam's cover.

But also using his contacts he got a job in Mexico City for his ex-wife, a nightclub chanteuse. Cast Claire Trevor. Her work permit listed as the necessary local address a P.O. Box in Cuernavaca.

P.O. Boxes in Mexico were all but impossible to trace. The postal officials were surprisingly officious and anyway the box was rarely in the name of the actual user. However, in this case we already knew this box.

I also had the ticket on a federal fugitive out of Chicago, charged with Crime Aboard Aircraft-Assault. Wealthy guy, no known Mafia connection, had attacked a stew, not a garden-variety crime. He was known to have a home in the swank Rancho Tetela section of Cuernavaca, and P.O. Box 123. I knew a lot of people in Rancho Tetela, and it was easy to locate Señor Andy, but getting him out was going to be a problem. He was legally in Mexico and had no criminal background. In the event he surrendered himself on the advice of his attorneys.

My contacts now advised me that a small, balding gringo named Señor Sam was now at the house. Sam de Palma. I had already documented this alias. Bingo.

If you don't find this stuff fascinating then I surely am not doing my job.

I shot a cable off to Chicago to interview Señor Andy. This was critical stuff, he obviously had sold the place to Sam, large money had changed hands. All this was crucial to a later prosecutive package. Nada. Chicago didn't even interview him. Very strange.

Meanwhile with my usual sputtering punctilio I had officially notified the Mexicans of Sam's background, and now of his location. He had been circularized and could not legally be in Mexico. Living in Cuernavaca under an alias was a gross violation of Mexican law. But I made no requests, I was perfectly happy to know where he was and have some good coverage on his activities.

I reported all this to FBI HQ and Chicago and next thing you know there was a foto of the place in Life Magazine. My foto. I sure as hell didn't send it.

This was way too much attention so Señor Sam moved. Moved to another mansion in Cuernavaca, child's play to find him in this tight community. Magnificent place, room to practice chip shots behind the ancient walls. Again I reported this to FBI HQ, Chicago and the Mexicans. But no fotos, let Life send their own people.

I was quite content with this situation but it had to be embarrassing to the Mexican government. Such a decision would be up to the Secretary of Government, the most powerful man in the cabinet, and it would be unthinkable that he would not consult the president. Hard to imagine that several Mexican presidents countenanced this situation.

This case was replete with strange episodes.

I developed the name of his Mexican manservant, a potential gold mine of information. Then I found that Pedro had emigrated to the U.S., even better. Pedro would know everything about Sam's life, his travel his calls, his friends, everything.

It was very difficult for a young Mexican male to get an immigrant visa. That is why we have the immigration people. I personally had sponsored thousands of visitor's visas, all carefully monitored, gaining good will and saving the Visa section time. I had never sponsored an Immigrant Visa, even the State people were wary in this area.

Pedro had gotten a visa to work as a servant for Kitty Kallen, once a famous singer and a pal of Sam's. The visa had personally and officiously been waltzed through the visa section by the Labor Attaché, very unusual. I had a lot of friends among the visa clerks and they remembered stuff like this. Very strange.

So I shot a cable up to Newark. Couldn't wait for the reply, key to the candy store. Pedro had to know the most intimate details of Sam's life, his body servant for years. Weeks later a one paragraph reply. Jess I work for Señor Sam, ver nice man, don know nothin.

I scortched back a screamer, get a more experienced agent, get a grand jury, get something. Nothing.

There used to be a song "If you love me in Oaxaca like you did in Cuernavaca, adiós". Now it was adiós Cuernavaca.

It was one of those pristine primavernal mornings found only at altitude in the tropics. The snow-crowned volcano peaks stood etched against the crystal sky dodging the dancing clouds. Beauteous birdsong belied the captivity of the cantor. The fragrance of lush foliage fought shyly with the aroma of fresh mountain coffee.

El patrón was in his pajamas and robe, enjoying the coffee, the view, his estate, his life. The ama de llaves (mistress of keys, great language or what) apologetically approached to advise that there was a young man at the portal who insisted on speaking personally to el patrón, the master. What now. Doubtless another charity. He went to the massive, carved, embossed, filigreed front and only gate to this colonial fortress.

The well-dressed young attorney was not conversant in English and Sam's Spanish was halting but it was clear that Sam was supposed to accompany him on some sort of official government business. Impossible. He would return inside, get dressed, call the well-known Attorney Fulano de Tal, friend of presidents, and straighten out this matter pronto.

Before he knew what was happening the dazed and ordinarily dapper don was in the San Antonio airport, still in his pajamas, being handed a summons by a U.S. Marshal. It was a summons to appear before a Federal Grand Jury in Chicago. It was a death sentence.

I wish I could claim credit for orchestrating this operetta. Alas, I was but a spear bearer. I don't know who designed this dramatic denouement. Perhaps the Presidente de México awoke in the night and said enough already, basta ya.

But I don't think the president of Mexico gave a flying frijol about Sam.

Gobernación called me and gave me the itinerary, relayed to FBI HQ and Chicago. By some miracle of organization a summons was issued and a U.S. Marshal in shining armor was awaiting Sam on his arrival in San Antonio.

I can't imagine what Sam was expecting at this point, probably arrest. Certainly not to be standing in the middle of a busy concourse in his pajamas staring at a bit of paper and searching his robe for a quarter to make a call. Somebody was going to pay for this outrage.

But he had already been positioned on the complex chessboard.

He had to appear before the grand jury or an arrest warrant would issue. Check. Upon appearance he would be asked about the Mafia. He could refuse to testify, claiming the Fifth Amendment. Castle. Whereupon the government would immunize him, he could not be prosecuted but must testify or go to jail. Queen's check. Appear and testify or go to jail for contempt. Sam had been through this ballet before. He had said he wasn't going back to jail, Checkmate.

Sam's body was found in the kitchen of the basement of his modest Chicago bungalow. Shot in the head by someone he knew and trusted. Someone who knew the basement wasn't bugged.

Not a bad way to go, couple of .22 slugs in the brain box while preparing some sausage and peppers for a trusted compadre, Italian peanut butter and jelly.

He said he wasn't going back to jail.

Richard Scalzetti Cain

Another great name. A real one, no pseudonyms this trip. And the name was very significant. Cain claimed that his mother was from Sicily and that was the reason he came to be accepted by the Mafia. Sam Giancana certainly seemed to have a lot of confidence in him.

He was as colorful as they come. Good-looking guy, mid-thirties, trim, blonde, sharp dresser, glib, confident, Mr. Cool from Corleone. Cast Dan Duryea. He had a fantastic past but a dodgy future.

He had been Chief of Detectives of the Cook County Sheriff's Office, which says a lot about Cain and about Cook County. It would appear he was already moonlighting for the Mafia. He was a heavy suspect in the death of a narco informant whose identity he learned through his position. He was not prosecuted but this crimped his career in law enforcement.

While still on the force he had made some semi-official trips to Mexico and made some good contacts. He spoke some Spanish and held himself out to be an authority on the Mexican scene.

Therefore he was ideal to coordinate Sam's Mexican honeymoon.

Cain and I had yet to meet but we had run into one another. Phyllis MacGuire of the famous MacGuire sisters was one of Sam's honeys. She was on one of her trips to rendezvous with her unlikely, unlovely, reportedly impotent and abusive lover. Cain was doing countersurveillance sweeps of the swank Hotel Maria Isabel. We continued to circle and sniff over the years.

Ironically it was a slip by Cain that led us to Sam. He had given Sam's P.O. Box as the local address for his ex-wife.

Cain may not have been a made Mafioso but he undoubtedly had access to a lot of good information and it soon developed that he was on the market. He contacted me and we had a number of meetings. He set the time and place, terrible tradecraft on my part. We met in a seedy bar on Melchor Ocampo, backs to the wall.

He was an interesting, intelligent, entertaining guy, but I really didn't enjoy being around him all that much. I kept expecting to see a black 1930s Buick bristling with tommy guns.

One night while I was there he drank 14 rum and colas. Maybe it was to honor the MacGuire sisters. No, wait, that was the Andrews sisters. That much sugar and caffeine and booze would have any normal person bouncing off the walls. Not Mr. Cool.

He had a nutty proposition. He claimed that he had worked for the FBI in Chicago for a couple of months and was paid $2000 a month and wanted a similar arrangement. Specifically he wanted a contract for a year at the salary of an active FBI Agent, then about $20,000. Why not a badge as well? In return he would shop Sam and the mob.

A man with Cain's experience would have known that Hoover wouldn't authorize this much for Giancana's privates on a platter with parsley. Hoover would sooner walk the Kennedy dogs over for a chat with Martin Luther King than pay such a price.

Personally I thought it was a bargain but doubtful that Cain ever would or could deliver. He certainly wasn't offering any samples.

I thought it was quite possible that this offer might come to the attention of the mob. I felt there was a leak at FBI, Chicago. Then again it might have been orchestrated by the mob as a test. Paranoia takes the policeman down strange paths.

The offer was duly forwarded and duly and properly dismissed. FBI HQ said Cain had never worked for the Chicago office. I don't know who was the liar.

If there had been a witness protection program something might have been worked out. I think he was living a fantasy and we both had seen too many gangster movies.

He lived it to the end. He returned to Chicago and one fine day was shotgunned to death on the street. One fine day is the annual average for Chicago. I don't think it was ever solved. When was a Mafia hit in Chicago solved?

Cain should have gotten out while he was able.

The True Cross

It is impossible not to fall in love with the romantic port of Veracruz, where the insolently brave Cortés began the conquest that changed the Americas forever. Veracruz is a complete culture in itself, a distinct dialect, renowned cuisine, a felicitous musical style played around the world, handsome, happy natives who often actually wear colorful regional costumes, a tropical spirit and gayness especially evident at carnival time. The approach over the incredibly green mountains or from the Gulf with views to the volcanoes is spectacular. The city itself is a wonder, colonial arcades, Spanish forts, docks, public markets, street musicians and the famous coffeehouses.

I loved Veracruz. I just didn't plan to go there that night.

We received very good information that the girl friend of a badly wanted bank robber would be arriving by plane that night. This presented problems. Normally we would work with Mexican Immigration or the Judicial Police at the airport, but they had little surveillance capability. If the subject weren't actually there waiting for her we were out of business.

So we decided to cover the arrival ourselves, not strictly kosher. As soon as they give you a badge it's an awful temptation to play cops and robbers.

Of course we had no radios or real surveillance capability either but we thought we could cover her arrival. She had to follow a fairly fixed path through customs, immigration and arrivals and airport transportation, and there was really only one route into town and little traffic at that hour. Once we knew her hotel more detailed coverage could be established.

So several of us went out to the airport in our cars and we managed to muster some contract investigators, good lads.

Everything went like clockwork. We had no problem following her arrival. She was a tall, pretty, stylish lady, which was a help. Those bank robbers had a way. Bonnie had come to meet her Clyde.

No one was waiting for her. She cleared the formalities and boarded a cab. One of the sources managed to jump in with the driver and give him some load of cow caca in Spanish. The cab took off for town with us in discreet pursuit.

About a mile from the airport the road merges with the main road to the center, the Viaducto. There is also an option to turn left to Puebla but nobody ever went to Puebla. They turned left. We had all already committed to the Viaducto and there was no turnaround for miles. Adiós. We tried but couldn't catch up.

I drove back to the office and glumly spent the rest of the night waiting to hear from our source. It was not impossible that they might shoot him. Clyde would have.

He called about dawn. The lady got in the cab and told the driver "Veracruz". 264 miles away from the capital. That was like arriving at JFK and telling the cabby Columbus, meaning Ohio, not Avenue.

The rest of the scenario rolled past the cameras without a hitch. The cab took the lady to a hotel in Veracruz where the subject was awaiting her. Presumably they spent a perfect night in this tropical paradise.

Mexican Immigration was alerted and rapidly organized a team and soon the whole package was on its way to the border, Bonnie, Clyde and the booty.

In the years ahead he no doubt treasured memories of that magical night. Gets tears when he hears "La Bamba".

Body Surfing in Acapulco

Living and working in Mexico was a wonderful experience but I hated working Acapulco. Stateside agents envied me this assignment but it was a terrible place to work. It was hot, dirty, fetid, lawless and disorganized. Supposedly it was the murder capital of the world, leaving a lot of bodies about, sometimes norteamericano bodies.

Another late night call. Another apparently American body found on the beach. Some damn news service reported it might be the body of James Earl Ray, the assassin of Martin Luther King. We chased phantoms of Ray all over Mexico.

The Chief of Police of Acapulco at this time was Metro Moon. Helluva guy. Probably had only killed 30-40 people in the line of duty. He was a pretty crafty and polished operator, perfect for the time and place. I had a lot of respect for Moon and consulted with him frequently in his office at the foul old jail.

Many times such consultations were very confidential in nature. I noticed there seemed to be a closet door in the office but paid it little mind. One day some flunky came in and opened the door and it was the Black Hole of Calcutta, jammed to the ceiling with sweating, stinking, fearful bodies. It was the holding cell from hell and they could hear everything said.

I contacted Chief Moon and begged him to preserve this body until it could be examined by an expert being flown down from Washington. The Acapulco police had no lab capability whatsoever, they could barely muster a telephone.

Law in the tropics demands immediate interment but I thought Moon might stretch a point.

I met the FBI lab expert at the Acapulco airport and drove him directly to the morgue, just as night was falling in the typically dramatic tropical way. The morgue was a little shabby peeling shack in the middle of the cemetery. The only light was a cobwebbed 40-watt bulb. The place was attended by an extremely surly watchman. Talk about spooky.

On a slab in the morgue was a smelly mound. Something was distinctly wrong here. The chief had ordered the body preserved and this had been taken to mean dump quicklime over it. Elsewhere murderers use quicklime to prevent identification.

Ni modo, the expert, fresh off a long flight, still in suit and tie, dug in. I was faux macho in those days and held the flashlight for awhile but soon gave up and went outside. The lab guy must have been in that room an hour before finding enough to convince him that this could not be James Earl Ray.

If it had been up to me 30 seconds in that room would have been enough to convince me that this could not be our man.

But lab guys are stalwart stuff. I put him back on a plane, don't think he ever took off his tie. I think his name was Bonebreaker, seriously. He didn't seem any happier with me than the watchman.

Preservar, conservar, enterrar, refrigerar, easy language or what.

Chief Moon called me about another body found on the beach. This appeared to be a young American whose skull had been crushed with rocks. The body was found at Pie de la Cuesta, an idyllic palm-fringed movie set beach, thatched huts a few miles and a few centuries from the glitz of Acapulco. The place was compellingly beautiful but plenty dangerous.

The young gringo had left a diary and the Chief wanted a translation. It was about the saddest saga one could imagine.

Upon his discharge from the military full of piss and navy beans he had bought a monster motorcycle and set out on a splendid adventure south. He was going to record everything in his diary as the first step toward Hemingwaydom.

He had a perfectly miserable time in the few weeks remaining to him. Mexican mountain roads were no place for a novice biker. He got caught in horrible storms and the damp journal recorded his terror. He finally landed in the tropical paradise of Pie de la Cuesta. But the natives were restless. They seemed covetous of his possessions. His last entries show him to be very worried about his situation.

With the diary we were able to identify him and notify his family. It was also easy to identify and prosecute his killers. They were still sporting his leathers.

Biker drag wasn't all that common on the beach at Pie de la Cuesta.

Georgia on my Mind

A fugitive was heading for Mexico in a fancy Mercedes with a trunk full of priceless paintings. The paintings had been pilfered from a collection in California. The fugitive was a young man who had worked as houseboy in the mansion housing the collection. There was some sort of relationship between the owner and the houseboy and I didn't envy the prosecutor.

Civilization was in no peril from this young art lover but there was a very real danger and fear that he would be able to dispose of the paintings and they would be lost forever. In a sense they were public property since the mansion had some sort of museum status.

It was a small but wonderful collection. For example, there was a stunning Georgia O'Keefe mission done in chalk which any collector would covet. Hang it over the sofa, no the color ain't right.

I started round the galleries and sure enough our friend had been by just a bit earlier with his portfolio of paintings. These were obviously authentic and not yet on any stolen list but he found no takers. As I discovered time after time, professional people in Mexico were as professional and correct as any in the world.

The collection included a number of small charcoal sketches by Diego Rivera, simple but beautiful things. He trotted them by the Galerias Mizrachi. As it happened Mizrachi had bought these sketches himself directly from Rivera and could easily identify them. Would have been a helluva witness.

The subject was headed for Acapulco. Fish in a barrel.

I had a lot of good contacts in Acapulco and one of them, an artist himself, located the subject in no time. There was only one street and the Mercedes stood out like a Gioconda in the Gents.

The whole package, fugitive, car and paintings, were on their way to the border within 24 hours. I got to sneak a peek at the art. Beautiful things, especially the O'Keefe, just stuffed in the trunk but complete and unharmed.

Everyone was overjoyed, the supervisor at FBI HQ, the California authorities, the Mexicans, the museum and the insurance people. It was nothing, a pleasure to work.

It was a piece of pastel.

Corazón de León

Corazón de León, so sonorous it is a song title, means Lionheart. The original Richard Lionheart was held hostage in the middle ages and only released on payment of ransom. The American government has a policy against ransom payments, rot away Richard.

Terry Leonhardy, the American Consul General in Guadalajara, had been kidnaped. I had served with Terry in Mexico City and liked and respected him. He was pretty much a paragon officer. And besides, he had this great name. There was some carping that he should have been more careful but this was pretty much caballo ca ca. We were all constantly advised to be on guard and change routes but there were only so many alternatives. I think a well-planned snatch, like a well-planned assassination, is all but impossible to prevent.

I was sent out to coordinate the investigation from the American end, and arrived just as Terry was released and returned home.

I was not privy to the negotiations leading to the release. Mexicans tend to be more pragmatic and less prissy in such matters. There was a story that a relative of a Mexican president had been kidnaped in Guadalajara and demands were made for the release of political prisoners. Instead, supposedly, the Mexican Army rounded up some more reds and let it be known that all would be shot unless the victim was returned.

It was late and Terry was understandably shaky but determined to be interviewed. He was blindfolded the entire time but this very intelligent, very articulate professional had kept careful mental notes during his captivity and was anxious to get this information to work. It was a bravura performance under extreme stress. I am still impressed.

And it was very helpful stuff. He had tried to keep track of the route but that was very difficult. However, once in his place of confinement there were several audible clues with enormous potential. He heard church bells. There are a million churches in Guadalajara. But he heard trains, there are only two main rail lines. He heard trucks down-shifting, Guadalajara is fairly flat.

All we had to do was follow the rail lines to an underpass or declivity near a church and then go house to house. Presumably the kidnappers would have departed but there would almost certainly be lead material.

I banged out the cables and English and Spanish versions of the interview. The Mexicans got the Spanish version to study and we were to rendezvous the next morning to start the search. I couldn't wait to get started.

The President of Mexico was deeply and personally interested in this case. When the Mexican President takes a strong position mountains move. All the top cops had been sent to Guadalajara, with their key aides, reps from the Federal Judicial Police, the Secret Service, the Federal Security Directorate, the State and City police. I had worked with most of them and knew them to be effective. But it was a lot of chiefs.

We met the next morning in the fine hotel they had chosen for HQ. I expect the hotel took a beating in the accounting department, they just about took it over, straining communications and room service.

After a conference over croissants we hit the road. I expected to find the hideaway well before noon.

As command vehicle someone had commandeered a luxury motor home, the only vehicle that could accommodate us all. I expect a couple of American pensioners were staring at the stumps which had anchored their beloved RV to the trailer pad.

The idea was to follow the railroad tracks until we found an intersection near a downgrade and a church. We attempted to drive parallel to the tracks but it wasn't possible. City planning pretty much died out with the Aztecs. It was a constant series of zigzags. (There is, I swear, a Spanish verb, zigzaguear.)

Each intersection required a decision. One comandante would order a left, another a right, and the driver would like as not let the RV follow its large nose. I was astonished at his dauntlessness in front of all this brass.

This went on the whole weary day. From time to time we would find a likely intersection and everyone would pile out and scour the surrounding area. Especially for a basement, Terry said a basement and they were rare. It was amazing how many such intersections we found. Guadalajara is a huge city.

Finally we all returned to the hotel. A futile day.

The next day there was a technological upgrade.

They got a huge helicopter from the Mexican Air Force. It seemed a good idea. The pilots were very impressive, U.S. trained. Another conference and charts and maps and all the comandantes charge out to the chopper to get a window seat.

Again I started the day full of optimism. How could we fail? We started flying along the rail lines, looking for the fabled intersection. It sounded unique but there is heavy truck traffic everywhere in Mexico. And churches. The early Spaniards wanted to buy a place in heaven the worst way. The worst way was to enslave a bunch of indians to build a church.

There was too much noise for the pilot to hear all the shrieked instructions but he also had a whimsical bent. We would follow the rails a bit and then he would veer out into the countryside. All my companions, known to me as capable men, were contentedly gazing at grazing goats.

Finally, exasperated, I would pound the pilot on the back of his fashionable flight jacket and motion the way back to town, to the iron horse. We would follow the rails for a bit and then back to the barren hills.

It began to be clear that they didn't really want to find anything. I was cast in a bad movie and given no script. All day long that frustration and that whoopwhoopwhoop. My companions seemed to be having a great time, "B" ticket ride.

Back at the hotel the congratulatory hugs were a little less ursine. Another day wasted. And then another. Finally everyone drifted back to their regular assignments. It was six months before they found the cellar.

I never did figure out the scenario. These jefes were no fools. It had every appearance of a smoke screen with the gringo for a witness. Maybe it was part of the release package. I don't know what happened to the kidnapers. I would wager they are all dead by now. They might have been dead then.

The comandantes didn't fare so well either. One shot his mistress and then himself. Another died in jail in Texas, choked on a peanut butter sandwich. Sure. Extra chunky. Another was indicted in California for car theft. I offered to be a character witness. Maybe then he would have told me what the hell was going on.

The Spy Who Came Down With A Cold

Counterespionage, detecting spies, ate up enormous resources for precious little product. Hoover and the brass, especially Sullivan, were enraptured with all this clandestine choreography. Hundreds of promising men were channeled into this work and spent their careers schizophrenetically searching for specters. Most of us tried to dodge this duty. It was almost a guarantee of a sentence to a major city, slow bankruptcy with boils on your ears and butts.

It was Hoover's proud and frequent boast that the FBI had thwarted Axis penetration efforts in WW II. Basically this was a handful of losers shoved off a submarine who lost little time in turning themselves in and were hanged for their pains. In fact in reviewing the literature one finds that most spies are espontáneos and practically have to beat down the door to get themselves recruited.

The security people tended to look on the criminal agents as stodgy stooges who storefronted for the really important stuff. I was a card-carrying criminal agent so mostly I got out of this heavy-duty dirty work.

Once for some strange reason I was booked into an advanced espionage course at Quantico. Everyone griped about Quantico, but I enjoyed it. Two weeks with pay in a lovely setting, regular hours, no calls, no deadlines. Summer camp. I had done the firearms and defensive tactics instructors' courses and now here I was with the spooks.

Actually there was a lot of interesting stuff, outlines of current important cases presented by dedicated and impressive men. I couldn't help noticing that a lot of dynamite information was being discussed in an old barracks that could have been bugged by a kid with a soup can and a kite string.

I kept my peace, these were security specialists. I had already blown my fragile cool by referring to MI-5, Brit security, as M-One-5.

I could tell you more but then I would have to kill you.

Whilst dozing through these top-secret tales I heard references to a promising case that was developing in Mexico. Mexico City was my turf, I was relief supervisor on both desks and would have thought I knew every case in the office. Good tradecraft, compartmented, need to know.

In the middle of all this I was pulled out of class to fly back to Mexico and provide protection for an LBJ visit.

I forgot about this case until I was assigned as alternate agent. There had to be an alternate for every source as a backup and over time I was alternate on nearly every source in the office. This was a huge headache because it meant many more file reviews and clandestine meets in the middle of a busy schedule.

It was also personally troublesome because I knew that when the commies took over, as they inevitably must given the nature of the opposition, they would pierce my claims to being a simple criminal agent and go right to the dental drill. I knew I would cave in at the threat of a careless manicure.

But I was eager to review this matter since I had heard all about this marvel from the illuminati in Washington. I checked out the several volumes from the special section of the musty vault and prepared for a good read.

There was nothing there, absolutely nothing. This guy had been on the hob for years and there was not a shred of positive or useful information.

In a way this was a huge relief because the major worry in these cases is that the source is an opposition plant, a double or triple agent. No worry here. If the opposition was stringing us they would have put at least some bait on the hook. This guy had furnished nothing.

I reviewed the stuff and met the guy several times, after the appropriate adagios. In the dark in the park if there is a mark on the bark, all that crafty crapola so dear to the hearts of those who would practice to deceive.

Real nice guy, bright and agreeable and eager. And well placed, in a position where he was in contact with and had gained the confidence of the opposition. But nothing seemed to ever come his way.

He was like a lot of people in this dodge, he just liked the cloak and dagger. He liked to cha cha cha to the Third Man Theme.

Post Script

I mentioned I was pulled out of class to fly to Mexico and provide security for LBJ. LBJ was making an official visit to Mexico and apparently Hoover had offered to provide extra FBI security for the visit, so Spanish-speaking agents were mustered from all the border offices and flown to Mexico.

One poor sod, a friend of mine, had the temerity to ask if he should take his firearm. Well this bounced up the bureaucratic chain and landed on Hoover's desk, and resulted in an explosion. Of course they should take firearms, they are FBI Agents on duty, do I have to decide everything around here.

Well of course they couldn't take firearms. They couldn't even board the international flights with firearms without special arrangements and a flock of armed foreign agents swarming in would be an unacceptable flouting of Mexican sovereignty. Who was going to tell Hoover? Nobody, that's who.

Not that it mattered. They had no cars or radios either and would get lost if they wandered more than a block from the Embassy. So they strolled around looking for anyone with "Assassin" stenciled on his T-shirt and flew back home.

LBJ was unscathed and appreciative. He and Hoover were old pals.

My Toughest Case

So what was my toughest case? The really big one where I took on the forces of darkness and triumphed.

Every office had a bank of junk cases used to bloat the meaningless statistics. In Mexico these were the Mexican fugitive cases. There were thousands of these cases. A lot of them were Escaped Federal Prisoners. Sounds like a big deal. No jail will ever hold me copper. Often as not it would be a homesick alien farm worker walking away from a road camp. Regular Dillinger. Others were Parole Violators and Bond Default, often for the same sort of crime.

Mexico City didn't even have to cook up these cases. The responsible office of origin was usually some border office, often without a prayer of locating the guy, who usually had returned home to Mexico.

Origin would send the lead to Mexico City, which would open a case, assign the leads and very often find the guy. And then find him again the following year in the same place. And every year report finding hundreds of fugitives. Beautiful. Well done, mighty manhunters.

The only flaw was it was a totally meaningless exercise. Nothing was going to be done. Mexico would not even consider delivering her own nationals to the gringos. Even if she did American immigration, in most cases, would not even consider admitting. Even if they did it would only be to parole them in for completing the expensive prosecutive process which would end in deportation. Back to Mexico.

Even in the case of a real badman, a drug dealer or murderer, Mexico would not send her citizens north, even under extradition procedures. They could and would sometimes prosecute in Mexico for extraterritorial crimes, but that is another story, lucky for you.

These cases were never assigned to me but they annoyed me because they were an exercise in futility and they used resources that could have been expended on real cases.

I was a criminal relief supervisor for twenty years. Mothers don't raise your kids to be relief supervisors. It was all headaches of administration with none of the power or pay. It was supposed to be a step up the ladder but I never had a jefe who troubled to take this step nor a fellow relief supervisor who was promoted. It doubled your work and chances for censure and made your squadmates very surly. It was another of Mr. Hoover's little jokes.

One day I was sitting on the criminal desk in Mexico and the clerks rolled in this monster file for review. Volumes and volumes. A major case and I had never heard of it. Strange.

Escaped Federal Prisoner. But the fugitive wasn't American or Mexican and wasn't a criminal. He was in fact a medical doctor and displaced person. He was born in Danzig or someplace that disappeared in the war and had qualified as a medical doctor. But his papers had all been lost and he had no passport or nationality. Somehow he had made it to AMERIKA. Immigration found him and locked him up. He was illegal but there was no place to send him, man without a country.

While they were scratching their heads he walked away from a road camp and made his way to Mexico where he had been practicing medicine back in the hills for twenty years. We are spending tax money looking for Dr. Schweitzer.

Escaped Federal Prisoner. We had located and relocated him 20 times. This was one case the Mexicans would have processed for deportation, but they had never been consulted. American immigration would have been crazy to admit him. No prosecutor had ever been consulted.

I shot a lead up to Phoenix, they consulted the U.S. Attorney, case closed.

When the criminal jefe returned he was furious. This case was his pet, been good for a fugitive statistic every year for 20 years and be good for another 20 if the good doc survived.

I figured I had resolved the case, saved the government all kinds of time, money and effort and pissed off my bosses. Maybe there was something in this deskwork after all.

These cases were a torment to me for years. Endlessly locating and relocating Mexican fugitives in Mexico for no positive end. Mexico wasn't going to do anything about them and wasn't even consulted. Social consequence was nil, few were criminals of consequence and nothing was done anyway. And it was costly, agents were constantly being shipped in mostly to man these cases, which were actually investigated by the contract sources, some of the finest investigators and swindlers in the world.

There was no point complaining to the jefes, they loved these cases. Easy stats man. No point in submitting a memo, the jefes wouldn't clear it. No point in talking to the inspectors, whose actual job should be to shoot down such folly. These cases had historic approval. One ran the risk of being critical of a program presumably approved by the deity.

The solution came to me in the dead of night.

The Suggestion Program.

Hoover had belatedly installed a suggestion program and then characteristically demanded participation, not that he actually wanted any damned suggestions.

The beauty part of a suggestion was that it did not need supervisory approval, it went right up to the executive conference.

I crafted the suggestion with some care. Don't actively seek these people in Mexico. Put them on the lookout lists in case they surfaced in the U.S. and let them be routinely handled by the Marshal's service, where they belonged.

Both of my jefes hit the ceiling, I was messing with motherhood. One wrote a seven page, seriously, seven handwritten legal-size pages, argumentum against, most work he had done in years. I didn't care, my time was almost up, just forward the thing like it says in the manual.

It so happened that I was in Washington for conferences when the suggestion arrived. More unbelievable static, actual rage. Hey, if you don't like it vote it down.

But the times were changing. Jim Adams, a feisty little Texan with a lot of field experience, was running things. He read the suggestion, simple thing really, quizzed me about it in a positive fashion and approved it.

Best thing I ever did in the face of the most opposition. Easily saved the government millions over the years.

America Central

KABOOM. Huge explosion and very close. Rattled the walls and windows and shivered the shit out of my shaky timbers. It was late in the evening of a long day and I was taking refreshment with some Costa Rican officers in the police canteen in San José. Someone had detonated a large bomb just outside, obviously targeting the police, and the noise and concussion and smoke and smell were tremendous. Typical latino machos the cops rushed the blast site, I headed for cover.

The Central American road trip was not a particularly prized assignment. One was on the road almost constantly dealing with difficult cases in problem areas. Even where our contacts were honest and competent they were already swamped.

The agent handling Central America for years suddenly put in for retirement. I had been in Mexico City for 16 years and the clock was running down. The kids seemed to have grown and gone. It looked like an interesting, challenging assignment. My jefes were probably happy to have me out of their hair.

Because of the rather sudden, mysterious departure of my predecessor there was no opportunity for overlap or indoctrination. Cold turkey. Just as well, starting without any preconceptions. My dear father was of the pitch-em-off-the-pier school of swim instruction and now I was perfectly at home in the water, long as I have my bubble.

I had primary responsibility for Panama, Costa Rica and Nicaragua and secondary for Guatemala, El Salvador and Honduras, fascinating places. I had long wondered why these little countries had not formed a federation but they are amazingly disparate.

First thing was to review all the pending cases. The best part of being an FBI Agent was working cases. Basically you're on your own. It is all but impossible to actually supervise casework and the jefes don't even try. They just proofread the reports. A field agent is alone with his conscience. Especially in Central America.

Everyone seems to presume that FBI Agents are right wing. This is basically true but the assumption is insulting. FBI Agents tended to assume State Department people were left wing, perhaps true but also presumptuous.

It was infuriating to me over the years that the U.S. was so identified with corrupt despots like Trujillo, Marcos, the Shah, Somoza and Noriega. Partly this was because of their anti-communist stance. Also it was true because the U.S. has no monolithic foreign policy, pity the small power trying to deal with Carter and then Reagan. Also it was true because of the dumb turnover policy of the State Department and simple housekeeping. It is much, much easier dealing with a dictator.

My predecessor was notoriously right wing and obviously got along gangbusters with Somoza and Noriega. Part of our quid pro quo in working overseas was handling investigations for them in the U.S., Foreign Police Cooperation. Sticky.

If our own supervisors don't supervise us think of the poor ambassador with all these loose cannon cops running around. I can't imagine why all these political hacks want to be ambassador. It is a terrible, impossible job, trying to satisfy State, Congress and the President, supervise a couple of dozen competing agencies within the embassy and trying to achieve ends usually inimical to the host country. Add an impossible social calendar and an unhappy wife who drove you to try for the job in the first place. There is never a spare minute.

No ambassador wants these policemen running around but the President has ordered it and no one else is going to do this work. So then of course he wants to know what you are doing. I have been through this a half dozen times. The ambassador wants to review your work. Of course Mr. Ambassador. But there is an immense amount of cases and most are very dull indeed. Usually one or two presentations suffice.

The A List

Costa Rica, cited as the model of civilization, had become a notorious haven for Northamerican fugitives. I knew this in a general way when I applied for this assignment but did not know the magnitude. There were something like a dozen gringo fugitives residing in Costa Rica with apparent impunity, rather a scandalous situation for a small, friendly, civilized state.

My predecessor had been so incensed by this outrage that he had fired off a steamy memo for the Embassy and the Costa Ricans detailing the identities, locations and activities of these fugitives and, in effect, demanding action. Naturally he didn't clear this with anyone and proceeded to retire, confident he had done his best.

I was not looking forward to reviewing these cases.

I was particularly gloomy about the infamous Robert Vesco case, the most prominent name on the list. Vesco was a multimillion-dollar swindler with Nixon connections. He had sought and found refuge in several Caribe climes, moving on as it got too warm.

On taking this assignment I expected Vesco to be my number one headache. He had worlds of money and influence and I anticipated that I would be expected to get him out in some legal fashion.

Usually the first major problem with a fugitive was the actual physical location. No problem in this case. Hell, his manor was featured as a major attraction on the daily tourist tour, like it was Graceland. "On your right is the estate of the famous gringo Roberto Vesco, note the armed guards on the wall and the TV cameras tracking us, everybody smile."

Vesco made no effort to hide. His wife shopped in the super, the kids were in the class play, Ozzie and Harriet.

There was a huge file on Vesco, which I reviewed very carefully. He was a fugitive all right. He was a federal fugitive. But he was not a Bureau fugitive. I found, to my astonishment, that there were strict instructions from the Bureau to take no action regarding Vesco. The case was the province of the

Securities and Exchange Commission and the Bureau had bowed out.

Great news, very mysterious but very welcome. Except that here was Vesco's name featured prominently on our aide-memoire demanding action, exactly contrary to Bureau instructions. Costa Rica was very touchy on the Vesco business, there had been several free-booter plots to snake him out.

The next most prominent name on the list was my old friend Santos Trafficante, the Mafioso from Tampa. I sorta liked old Santos. For one thing he had the all time greatest name in gangster history. For another he was a good family man and was not known for stringing his minions from meathooks.

But Santos had returned to plague me. He had retired to Costa Rica. Again his whereabouts were no mystery, he was residing in a modest apartment in San Jose. He was listed with the government, a perfectly legal pensionado.

Again there was a huge file. Again I found he was not an FBI fugitive. Not a fugitive of any kind nor were there instructions about taking any action against him.

I couldn't wait to review the rest of the files.

It was imperative that I review all these cases of supposed American fugitives hiding in Costa Rica because the American Ambassador had summoned my boss and I to come to San José to defend this communication. The Ambassador was justifiably furious because no such communication had been cleared through his office and the Foreign Office was getting on his case.

A review determined that there were indeed some ten American fugitives known to be hiding illegally in Costa Rica, a fairly disgraceful situation. It appeared that my departed colleague, upset by this situation, prepared the list and then just threw in Vesco and Trafficante for good measured. What the hell, they had it coming, let the lawyers squabble about technicalities.

The Legal Attaché and I presented ourselves in the offices of Ambassador Todman at 9 AM as ordered and were told we were on our way to the Foreign Office. On the short ride, my only ride ever in a chauffeured embassy limo, the Ambassador advised me that I was to handle the presentation.

Great. Gives me about three minutes to prepare the defense of an indefensible, incorrect, improperly researched, offensive and unapproved memo. In Spanish. I didn't really enjoy the ride much.

In about five minutes we were ushered through the ornate offices into the august presence. Only time I ever met a Foreign Minister. Can't say I enjoyed it. Really can't remember much of what happened.

When I get real nervous the words just spew forth flecked with the foam of the truly frantic. I have no idea how long I was on stage. No one else spoke.

All this cha cha cha was in Spanish although the Foreign Minister probably spoke better English than we did and did so whilst waltzing Mrs. Vesco at the Presidential Ball.

Finally the ordeal was over and we were ushered out. It seemed to me some comment was called for but not a word was spoken on the way back to the Embassy. The Ambassador said nothing then or thereafter. The Legal Attaché said nothing on the long flight back to Mexico City. They seemed bemused.

A year later not a soul on the list was still in Costa Rica. Vesco moved on to other Caribbean venues. Trafficante returned on his own to Florida. The actual fugitives were either deported or surrendered themselves. A very sticky situation had been resolved. Perhaps from the memo, perhaps from the Ambassador, perhaps just the times.

Personally I think the Foreign Minister did not want to go through that exercise again. I know I didn't.

Miami Bound

I was asleep alone in my room at the Hotel Amstel in San José, Costa Rica. About midnight I was awakened by a call from the Marine Guard at the Embassy. Someone had called the Embassy claiming that he was wanted for bank robbery in Puerto Rico and wanted to surrender to the FBI. Hey! That was me.

I made a few fast calls to FBI HQ and San Juan and quickly confirmed that there was such an individual, a badly wanted fugitive on bank robbery charges. This was a BIG bank robbery, an armed assault with loot in the region of a quarter million dollars, a really big job. There were terrorist and nationalist overtones. The fugitive was a huge guy, over 100 kilos, considered armed and extremely dangerous. What fun!

The supposed fugitive called back several times. His speech was disjointed but he seemed to be the real article, name, rank and serial. He said he wanted to surrender but he had a set of conditions. He would surrender only to the FBI, Costa Rican authorities must not be notified and he must be returned to Puerto Rico directly. All these were pretty much impossible, there was no acknowledged FBI in Costa Rica, the Embassy would be constrained to operate with the Costa Ricans and there were no flights to Puerto Rico.

And it must be handled that night.

FBI HQ and San Juan were desperate to get this guy so I told him to come on in, we would try to comply with his demands.

My first thought was that this was likely a subterfuge for the Puerto Rican nationalists to gain entry for a high profile assault on the American Embassy. On the other hand we might never get such a chance again.

I cleared this with the Embassy Security Officer, a real ballsy guy, as they often were. We decided not to trouble the Ambassador.

The arrangement was I would wait for the subject just inside the outer door of the Embassy. I would make sure he was alone and unarmed before admitting him further. If there was any attempt to force entrance I would fling myself aside and the Marine would open fire.

There were only the two of us and I had no firearms, strictly forbidden. The Marine was perfectly agreeable but he had no firearms either in this peaceful post.

In the meantime I was exploring how to get our friend to Puerto Rico. There were no good connections.

I knew that the Royal Canadian Mounted Police had recently sent a DC-8 to Costa Rica just to transport a Canadian swindler home. The Mounties are notoriously cheap and swindlers are famously non-violent.

Simplest and safest to me seemed to be to charter a little twin from San Juan and have it waiting at the airport. Couple of hundred bucks and Bob was our uncle. But of course the Bureau wouldn't approve. Hoover had to approve anything over $50 and nobody was going to call him. Clyde got testy.

Meanwhile our friend showed up as advertised. Only he had an escort, some Costa Rican compadres. He looked like a hall of fame bandido but was unarmed and subdued. I let him in, the friends waited outside.

We conversed in Puerto Rican. I slapped a Miranda warning on him but he wasn't very communicative.

He was clearly the wanted man and admitted involvement in the bank robbery but no details. He seemed to be in a drugged torpor, which was just as well since he looked like he could walk through walls.

We passed what little remained of the night in the reception area under the eye of the gunless guardian. The Security Office offered to come help baby-sit but things seemed under control.

Early the next morning the duty driver drove us to the airport, where I knew there was an early flight to Miami, the only connection. Naturally the flight was fully booked. We were put on standby, me and the monster. Standby. Finally we got the last two seats. I don't even want to think about what the alternatives could have been.

The little LACSA flight lifted off punctually at 9 AM, completely full, three and three. The captain announces the flight time, 2 hours 45 minutes, a long, long time.

My guy isn't manacled or restrained in any way but he looks and acts weird and wired, sniffing and snorting and bobbing his head. I thought he was on drugs which could wear off at any time and there would be hell to pay. He could renege on his agreement at any time and I had zero authority to act.

The Captain proudly announced that we were flying over Cuba. Great. What if my pal takes the plastic knife from the food tray and holds it against our already nervous seatmate's neck and demands a landing?

While I am brooding about such possibilities our chatty Captain comes on the PA to request that the FBI Agent who is aboard with a prisoner come forward to identify himself. Ho Boy. Heads were spinning all over the aircraft. No question who was involved, the disheveled gringo and the frito bandido. All the others were serious Tico businessmen. Serious, nervous Tico businessmen.

Still, legalistically, I was an Embassy officer and the subject was not technically a prisoner, so I kept my peace. Maybe it would all go away. I didn't feel like abandoning my charge and traipsing up the aisle to explain this complex situation.

Things quieted for awhile and then another announcement in both languages. Will the FBI Agent with a prisoner identify himself to the Captain. This time my companion nudges me heavily with his elbow. Hey, dummy, he means you.

So I wearily and warily walk up front to the cockpit and try to explain to the captain, who has gotten an inquiry about the situation from Miami. Yes there is an Embassy official aboard with a gentleman with some legal problem, but there was no prisoner and should be no problem.

Prisoners are very special problems for airlines. The FAA required that Captains be notified and sometimes Captains refused to board prisoners. The Captain was a helluva nice guy who later became a pal, but he and I knew that he was carrying a hot potato.

The subject was technically not a prisoner and would not be until such time as he decided to unsurrender himself, which would place us in legal limbo, a popular Caribbean dance wherein one shuffles ever lower under the bar of justice.

Who knows where jurisdiction lay over a U.S. fugitive on a Costa Rican flight over Cuba?

I returned to my seat to the stares of my fellows and the approval of my compañero. Our seatmate mumbled "perdone, perdone, con permiso" and went up to the toilet. I hope they had seat belts in the crapper because he never returned.

Our Captain announces we will be arriving a little sooner than expected. About an hour sooner. In no time we are on the tarmac in Miami.

Normally on flights from Latin American chaos and disembarkation are simultaneous. By the time the seat belt sign flashes off the aisles are jammed with people loading up and shoving forward. Not this time. Everyone remained quietly and stoically belted whilst my friend and I strolled off to be greeted by a contingent from FBI, Miami.

The weird part is that all through this nightmare scenario I was never nervous and I get nervous having my teeth cleaned. The bandido went off to the jail, I never did learn the reason for his surrender. His Tico pals hinted there was a lady involved. What else?

I was commended for what I now realize was a foolish handling of a sensitive situation. As a result of this and other wonderful work I got a cable from FBI HQ naming me Legal Attaché, San José, a dream assignment. But with typical Hooveresque hubris no one had checked with the Ambassador. And he didn't want any more cowboys playing with his indians.

Across the Agua to Managua

In sharp contrast to San José and Panama I hated Managua. An earthquake had left the capital devastated, a company town gone bankrupt, abandoned by God and pillaged by Somoza. The Embassy was a fortress, my office was my lap. Local authorities were difficult. Even shelter was a problem, the only real hotel was bugged by Somoza. They charged more than per diem anyway, against my religion.

In reviewing the Nicaraguan cases I found to my distress that most of the caseload seemed to consist of leads relating to the Nicaraguan colony in California. Fair enough since there were lots of Nicaraguans in California. But most of them were anti-Somoza and most of these leads smelled political.

Most of the ambassadors and my predecessors had been pro-Somoza. We had fallen into covering leads in California for Somoza's feared G-2. This was unconscionable, these people all had relatives in Nicaragua subject to reprisal. There was a big volume of such cases and no oversight, no policy supervision. It was hopeless to ask my bosses or the inspectors for any guidance. The cases had the stamp of precedence, therefore sacrosanct.

I just unilaterally stopped forwarding the requests or the replies. The caseload dropped but no one seemed to notice.

Oh sure, may be coincidence but Somoza was gone in just a year or two.

Ring Around the Rositas

Major car theft rings were a big deal in the old Bureau. Lots of potential for recoveries and statistics and prosecutions and an answer to the critics forever carping about our working crap cases. But they were not a lot of fun. The prosecutors and public were not terribly interested. The housekeeping was a tedious headache. Car A stolen from victim B at point C transported to E, retitled at F and finally sold to G, multiply by twenty. All this has to be documented or the prosecution is out the window. This is triply troublesome in Latin America, especially since the authorities are almost certainly involved.

A Nicaraguan Customs official broke this ring single-handed. It was an immense undertaking. He had identified and seized a couple of dozen luxury cars stolen in California and marketed in Nicaragua.

Don Porfirio was a mid-level official in Nicaraguan Customs who suddenly found salvation in seizing stolen cars. He used to drive around Managua in his official jeep and spot these cars. Lord knows they were easy enough to spot in rag tag Managua. Big hairy Lincolns, Cadillac phaetons, sleek Mercedes ragtops, purring Jags, stood out like Tarzan at a tea party. He would get the numbers, I would verify they were stolen and he would roll them up.

He had a whole Customs' lot full of these beauties rotting away under the tropic sun.

He liked to have me drive around Managua with him in the official jeep. I hated to drive around with him in the official jeep. He had a big grudge and was morose company and this was a very dangerous business.

They couldn't have gotten all these buses into Nicaragua without some heavy influence, meaning Somoza. All the purchasers, from whom the cars were seized, claimed to be innocent third parties, which was hardly likely, and they all had to be influential also to even think of riding around in such splendor.

Porfirio had to be getting on a lot of nerves. Sure enough one fine day he was gunned down while approaching his home in the official jeep. Bullets all over the place. Machine gunned. Gory pictures in all the papers. As a lesson? Lesson to whom?

Everyone knew only the military had machine guns in those days.

Panama Cha Cha Cha

Panama City has that special tropical pizazz, like a combo of Vegas and Veracruz. It is a beautiful setting, the lush jungly mountains meeting the sparkling sea. It could be breathtakingly hot and humid or breezily pleasant. There were ample appalling slums and lots of luxury high rises. There were some wonderful colonial buildings in the center and great old double veranda barracks in the Zone.

There were very distinct worlds within worlds, the often shabby Republic, and the contrastingly ordered Zone and gringo bases. There were wonderful restaurants and super shopping opportunities, so rare in that time and area.

The Zone was like Oz, middle America magically transported intact to the tropics. Clipped lawns, Legion posts, movies and popcorn, high school hops. I loved the amenities of the Zone, clean and secure, fine police and public services, and I never tired of the mystique of the Canal.

There was a schizophrenetic shock crossing into Panama, a time warp, from "Our Town" to "Sadie Thompson". Most of the Zonians never made the trip.

The Embassy was in the midst of the treaty negotiations, which would transform forever this strange juxtaposition.

It wasn't an easy place to work. Drug Enforcement had recently lured a big trafficker onto the Zone for a softball game and arrested him as he thought he was sliding home. The Embassy wanted no further such antics. There were a number of leads involving fraud and the numerous storefront banks which ran afoul of the privacy laws.

The main mosca in the ungüento was that all leads were to be funneled through the now infamous Coronel Manuel Noriega, head of the National Guard and the main man. Nothing was to be done without clearing it through him.

My illustrious predecessor said this was no problem, but then he was in love with Noriega, if that can be imagined. There is, somewhere in the files, a letter from Coronel Noriega to J.

Edgar Hoover recommending that his amigo Sr. Brokenbed be made Legal Attaché to Panama.

Noriega and I didn't get along nearly so well.

The drill was that on traveling to Panama an appointment was to be made to confer with Noriega in his offices at the National Guard G-2, a seedy concrete complex down on the waterfront. I was waltzed through a series of insolent and immaculate Guardsmen, which is to say the exact opposite of the usual Panamanian, cordial and carefree.

After a long wait in the reception area, whose décor would have shamed a Belizean bordello, I was ushered into the presence. The same repugnant, pocked, heavy-lidded, snake-eyed villain we all came to know and loathe on TV, the personification of evil. I had dealt with many corrupt and uncooperative Latin law officers over decades. Nearly always there were redeeming graces, humor, charm, courtesy. This was a total thug from central casting.

I went through this unpleasant adagio a half dozen times. I don't know what was the problem. The FBI didn't make payoffs, which suited me fine but maybe not Noriega. It was like some maitre d' who seems to feel extra surliness will up the tip. So I just stopped dropping by.

The Embassy and Military were probably pleased to see me out of the loop. They had full time teams trying to keep track of this toad.

I could not believe that the U.S. launched an intervention when Noriega was completely out of pocket. Just like I could not believe that the U.S. would launch an intervention of Cuba without a certainty of success.

Where's My Transfer, Conductor?

Under the reign of Edgar the Terrible transfers were fearfully traumatic. Even a desired transfer cost thousands of scarce dollars and great hardship to the family. Edgar used transfers as Torquemada used tongs. What did he care, he lived his whole life in the radius of a long kite string. We had suffered ten moves in our first ten years and now it was time again.

The Bureau now had a rule limiting a foreign assignment to four years, aping similarly stupid State Department policies. The more experience on post the more potential effectiveness.

The usual transaction was to waive grade 14 in return for a transfer to a cherished office at grade 13. This sounded like nonsense to me, I didn't see any Colonels accepting a cut to Major to get Camp Pendleton. They didn't know what to do with me. Then transfers started arriving in clusters.

First I was transferred to San José, Costa Rica as Legal Attaché, grade 15, a dream assignment. Alas, not to be, nobody consulted the Ambassador.

Next a call from FBI HQ, would I be interested in Senior Resident Agent at Vista, California? Would Sly make movies if he had to take off his shirt? Alas, an inspection wiped out the post.

Another call from FBI HQ, would I be interested in Legal Attaché, London. Would Zsa Zsa marry a titled furrier? Legal Attaché, London, was our most pre-eminent and prestigious overseas post, the jewel in the crown.

How soon could I be there? Three days. I think it took a week including conferences in D.C.

Wrong Way to Tipperary

The London operation was not comparable in any way to the Mexican menagerie. London had a third the personnel of Mexico and handled three times more cases, none of them junk. The Legal Attaché in Mexico had no cases and a full time assistant and secretary and almost never left the office. In London I had over 100 cases, none of them junk, and was on the street every day keeping up contacts. And I couldn't begin to keep up with my assistants.

In Mexico I banged out several cables a day, thought I was cable king of the world. London dealt almost exclusively in cables, there was no time for reports, the normal meat and potatoes of the paper-obsessed Bureau. It was a very efficient way to operate. I loved it but it wore me out.

I was barely settled in at the funky old Landsdowne Club and could just about find my way to the Embassy when we got an urgent, very sensitive, lead in Ireland. Ireland and Scandinavia were also part of the turf. The assistants were swamped so I happily assigned the lead to your servant.

Flew over to Dublin and took the train traversing the storied green hills to the bleak and stormy Northwest coast. The lead was to make a clandestine contact with a federally protected witness, hiding out on this remote area where authorities were not terribly welcome. Apparently he had testified against the mob.

In contrast to nearly all our regular work this was to be done without consulting local authorities. The important thing was not to lead anyone to the witness, not even the authorities and especially not the mob.

It was a long but pleasant trip to the little coastal town.

I checked into the only hotel, the Station Hotel. These fusty old relics were a charming feature of travel in the islands.

The contact was accomplished with appropriate caution, countersurveillance and countersigns. This was a remote but extremely suspicious and watchful area. I think he only wanted a bit of hand-holding.

Content with a job well done I returned to the hotel for a welcome pint of Guinness and took a table at the appealing station restaurant. Food in the Irish countryside was reputed to be far superior to that available in Britain.

There was only one other group in the cozy restaurant. Obviously foreigners also. Large gentlemen, dressed in dark double-breasted suits, waving their hands and speaking in a foreign tongue. ITALIAN. Holy smoke. This was literally out in the middle of nowhere. Had I led the Mafia to their man?

A little discreet inquiry developed that there was an Italian stocking factory nearby and this was a meeting of the board. These guys wore the product on their feet, not their heads.

It was a wonderful meal, wonderful trip. Was this a great job or what.

The Met – Scotland Yard

The London Metropolitan Police, the justly famed Scotland Yard, occupies a unique position in Britain, encompassing jurisdictional grounds that would be covered by dozens of agencies in the States. The Met was one of the main reasons we were able to move such mountains of work. I was down there nearly every day. Their investigators had worlds of expertise, sophistication and pride. Their commanders were the most remarkable men I ever worked with.

We stressed and stretched the relationship a lot.

Edwin Wilson was the most frustrating fugitive case in my experience. He was a CIA renegade who had become a federal fugitive for arms trafficking and other charges. He had found refuge in Libya where he was dancing the Qaddafi quadrille. It would be hard to imagine a fugitive more inimicable to American interests than a former top CIA operative working for our worst enemy. A very, very dangerous man.

Wilson was from a poor farm family in Idaho. He worked his way through Catholic schools and became a Marine officer in Korea, where he was recruited by the CIA. A disturbing pattern among their turncoats.

By a combination of ambition and ability and demonic energy he became a real power in security circles in the D. of C. He brokered a number of arms deals and amassed a substantial fortune, sporting a mansion in the Virginia hills. But he went completely out of control and now was working for the opposition. He was a clever, manipulative man with plenty of funds and expertise in the clandestine world. A very tough quarry.

Lots of agencies were looking for him, not necessarily working together and not necessarily including his former associates.

He had all sorts of United Kingdom connections. His girl friend, his arms business, some properties. He was known to travel frequently to the U.K.

In hottest pursuit were two very active prosecutive teams from the U.S. There was a great bulldog team of federal prosecutors from Virginia and another competent and hard-charging team from the Manhattan District Attorney's office. Both had a lot of information on Wilson and both had very good sources, very good indeed. Sources they did not want to share, for very good reasons. The sources would be in mortal danger if word got to Wilson. Both teams came to London independently, hot on the trail of Wilson.

London had a plethora of official visitors, practically a plague. But believe me none of these people ever saw the sights, they worked day and night.

All this activity was to be coordinated with the Met, the ideal agency in all the world for this job. It was their turf, they had the pride and the people and plenty of jurisdiction and arrest power. This was cleared at the highest level and they happily assumed responsibility for the U.K. aspects, with the proviso that all actions were to be coordinated and cleared with the Legal Attaché.

The Met assigned crackerjack teams to the visitors and information was just pouring in, great stuff, bound to lead to an early apprehension.

It never happened.

Wilson had at least two safe houses in the U.K. He had a small hotel in the northern rail center of Crewe. The Yard people thought it would be difficult to identify and establish coverage of this property, with the usual disdain of the big smoke for the rustics. I knew the Crewe cops would already have sniffed out the place as suspicious. As proved to be the case. Coverage was easily established but Wilson never returned.

Similar coverage was also established on an office in London and his girl friend, with similar results. We were literally only hours behind him but no happiness.

It became clear that he had been tipped off. That was plenty bad enough, but of even more concern was the safety of the sources, who had been in intimate contact with Wilson, known to be a vengeful man. Later from behind bars he tried to put out hits on his wife and the federal prosecutor.

Late one evening after moving some of these gambits around Scotland Yard I got a call from the pre-eminent Assistant Director, not an everyday occurrence. He was very capable, experienced and respected, also a rarity at that altitude. But he was a pal of the Manhattan DA, who had gotten to him. He instructed me to insure that the Brits followed the Manhattan scenario. I had spent all day orchestrating efforts to promote the Virginia efforts.

I had to advise the Assistant Director that he was not in possession of the full facts. He had to instruct me that he was the Assistant Director. Not pleasant. Or productive.

I have no idea who tipped off Wilson. For a long time I thought it might have been his CIA cohorts. His arrest in London on arms charges could have been very embarrassing and maybe dinged some careers. However I have seen very little evidence that abject failure impinges on company careers. I made the mistake of checking with them. They said they had no information and no interest. Sure.

It could also have been the Crewe crew. Too many people knew about all this interest in the Yank in this small community. Wilson would have some sort of fail-safe. Or it could have been associates in London.

Whoever it was cost the governments untold resources and could easily have cost lives. Whoever it was was involved in prosecutable criminal conspiracy. If it was CIA it was a mare's nest.

It was a giant frustration and disappointment and a large factor in my decision to retire. Getting too old.

Some time later the U.S. Marshals in an absolutely wonderful sting that Hoover would never have approved, lured Wilson to the Dominican Republic and thence to durance vile in America. Must be hard time.

Read the other day that Wilson's main confederate Frank Terpil is in Cuba. Probably plays cards with Vesco.

Vetting

There I was again paralyzed with fear in front of a huge group of very experienced British officers. Somehow I had let myself be talked into addressing a conference on applicant matters. As usual the Brit drill was to haul a Yank up in front of a large crowd to embarrass himself by trying to explain the silly Yank way as opposed to the superior U.K. system. As usual, they were correct.

Applicant matters, everybody hated them. Who would join the FBI expecting to handle vetting. They were a morass of short deadlines which took precedence over real work and were a rich source of censure. However a lot of extra agents got signed up because of the volume of this work. Including your servant.

They were set up to try to keep spies out of sensitive jobs, the usual Bureaucratic butt cozy, locking the barn after Bossie was gone. The Brits had taken a terrible beating at the hands of the Camford poofs and were determined to guard against recurrence.

They set up groups composed of experienced, mostly retired officers, responsible for vetting. One officer would be assigned one applicant and work the case until he was satisfied.

By contrast the Bureau was to shoot leads all over the country and demand results in three weeks. Only rarely would a single Agent get a real handle on the applicant. It happened to me once, my only applicant major case.

It was for a cabinet appointment, which required much more depth in handling. The subject was a lawyer who had spent most of his professional life in Mexico.

I interviewed scores of people, most of them respected professionals. Because of his aggressiveness a lot of these people, including a former wife, did not like him. But all agreed he was extremely intelligent and competent. I turned in a 200 pager, probably a record, Mr. Guinness. It was a mixed bag but I personally thought he would make a superb executive. He flunked. Probably blamed me.

So I had worked hundreds, perhaps thousands of applicant matters and presumably had some expertise. As usual I prepared by not sleeping well and leaving the matter to the last minute and the adrenal glands.

I can only conjecture that the brilliance of the presentation left them thunderstruck. One lone American dancing on the edge of hysteria without falling off the stage. They were too stunned to even applaud or participate in the 60 minutes of Q & A which had been scheduled (pronounced like shed).

Johnny and Clyde, Hoover and Homosexuality

The public seems endlessly curious as to whether Hoover and his lifetime companion and confidant Clyde Tolson were lovers.

I certainly hope so. It is depressing indeed to think of them putting up with each other all those years without an occasional snuggle. There is a famous foto of Hoover focusing his Brownie at Clyde posed prettily on a bench in Florida. If that ain't a fella snapping a shot of his honey I'll kiss your coconut. There are several such fotos but nothing so flagrante as to scandalize your auntie.

Clyde Tolson was Hoover's alter ego and equally feared. He had come into the Bureau as a clerk and worked his way up to Associate Director in about a fortnight. So he had about the same amount of field experience as Hoover, a perfect match. Cartha "Deke" Deloach, the career Hoover apologist who had about the same career trajectory, claims that Clyde was manly, not pretty, and was first baseman on the FBI championship baseball team, so that pretty much takes care of that.

"Deke" in fact states that Clyde was more of a man than the author Anthony Summers, as he had seen them both at close quarters.

Summers was retailing a story by a lady who claimed to have seen Hoover in a dress. Highly unlikely, even them pleated slacks made him look fat.

"Deke" rehashes the legend that Hoover claimed to be in regular contact with an informant who was the madam of a whorehouse in Ciudad Juárez, Mexico. You bet. Just hope he wasn't wearing that tacky satin dress.

"Deke" thinks it significant to note that no one who knew Hoover well in the FBI has ever even hinted at such a charge. Bet your sweet biffy. As to Summers' claim the Brit officer Stephenson recognized them as a homosexual couple, "Deke" responds "I saw them together for decades and never concluded any such thing, nor did anyone else who knew then." So there. I would imagine that almost anyone would tend to this conclusion without knowing them at all. If it looks like a duck, quacks like a duck, and walks like a duck.

I had several prolonged tête-a-têtes (no, dammit, that means head to head) with both of these gentlemen and came away convinced that they were so divorced from reality that commonplace conclusions were immaterial.

My own feelings have long been that there are a lot of people whose libido has left them in limbo. I think there are many such people who have never engaged in homosexual practices and who would not acknowledge homosexuality. Some wear collars backwards. In fact, if one does not practice or acknowledge homosexuality, could one be considered homosexual?

I don't know if they were homosexual. "Gay" is not a word that leaps to the lips to describe either. They never made a pass at me.

But by golly they did walk like ducks.

We were all very relieved when Hoover's estate was settled to find that it was only around a million, a relatively modest amount for a single man with inherited D.C. property, no transfers and 55 years of service. Especially since he famously never spent a penny and had a half dozen best sellers written by staff.

It surprised no one that it all went to Tolson.

The Troll on the Grassy Knoll

We have come a long way, you and I, and we have come to know one another. If you have stuck it out this far you are entitled to know the true story of the Kennedy assassination. Endless polls over the decades establish that the overwhelming majority of people believe that it was the result of a giant conspiracy. Well, the people are right.

As part of the job in London we were expected to lecture regularly to the senior detective courses conducted by the Metropolitan Police. Very scary. Part of the drill was to show us into the empty auditorium first, explaining that otherwise the size might intimidate. Like the Romans showed the Coliseum to the Christians, so they wouldn't be nervous.

A grizzled dick is daunting. These were the most experienced investigators in the best police department in the world and they believed there was a conspiracy. I convinced some of them and maybe I can convince some of you.

Like everyone I can recall where we were when we heard the sad news. We were traveling across the sere Mexican deserts en route for home leave. The kids were distraught. The golden-haired girls had actually met the fabled president prince at an Embassy garden party.

Although I did not know it at the time, there were puzzling Mexican ramifications. Oswald had made a mysterious trip to Mexico City and been in contact with the Soviet and Cuban Embassies. Frustrating man-years were to be spent on this aspect of the investigation.

I am not an expert on the assassination and was not in the mainstream of the investigation, but I spent many thousands of hours working on the case and knew and respected many of the lead investigators, top men. After a very shaky start it became a very thorough, professional probe, unparalleled in history. The Warren Commission did a tremendous job, bulldozing the Bureau into another dimension of inquiry.

I used to try to keep up with the conspiracy literature, but that is hopeless.

Certainly the case is replete with puzzling and disturbing circumstances, anomalies, coincidences, irrationalities, all anathema to the investigator. But equally unappealing to the conspirator. The whole point of a conspiracy would be to present a plausible plot, to deflect any thought of a conspiracy.

The marksmanship was remarkable. Well within the range of feasibility, but a conspirator would be asking a lot of the marksman. The junky, easily traceable rifle would be an atrocious choice for the conspirator. The ballistics are a puzzlement but bullets famously follow strange trajectories and certainly no conspirator can plan such paths.

I was and am troubled by Oswald's Russian idyll. I can't believe that the Russians would not have targeted him for recruitment. Vastly more material on this visit is surfacing daily and none of it supports a conspiracy.

I am troubled by Oswald's association with the emigré group in Dallas, his Fair Play for Cuba antics, and his trip to Mexico. He was a strange man. Nearly all regicides are strange loners.

Perhaps you wish to believe that the conspirators arranged for Oswald to seek and get a job at the Texas Book Depository because it offered a vantage point from which to snipe at a president whose very visit and itinerary were problematical.

I agree with the Oliver Stone critic who opined that such a conspiracy would have required the collusion of about two million co-conspirators. In fact I agree with all Oliver Stone critics.

I am not an expert on the assassination but I am something of an expert on the capabilities of our intelligence agencies. I fear they are not capable of successfully organizing to fix a senior slow-pitch softball game.

I think this convinced some of the Brits. They had worked with the Brit security services. Did they consider these services capable of such a conspiracy? Certainly not. They didn't consider them capable of crossing the street.

This convinced some of them. But wait. The argument is that this could not be a conspiracy because it was so inept. At the same time the man says it couldn't be the intelligence agencies because they are too inept. Couldn't an ept agency plan an inept effort precisely for this purpose? Round like a circle.

I have brooded over this for years and certainly don't expect to convince any grassyknollistas. Believe what you like.

PS

Data becoming available from the Freedom of Information Act and from the former USSR enables us to reconstruct the scenario of the conspiracy. The plotters are grouped around the conference table in the soundproofed room. The chairman speaks.

003 you are to recruit some nut who is a Marxist and a marksman. After suitable indoctrination send him to Dallas to get a job in a building overlooking Dealy plaza. Have him send Dealey for some cheap, shoddy, easy to trace mail order rifle.

004 you arrange to have Kennedy make a trip to Dallas where everyone hates him and parade through this plaza.

005 get a spent bullet from this bum rifle and leave it on the stretcher afterward.

006 arrange with the Mafia to have Ruby kill Oswald afterwards at Police Headquarters.

Murphy, you go for coffee and Danish.

Everyone set? Synchronize watches. Remember, mum's the word. No No, Murphy, nothing to do with your mother.

About the Author

Richard S. Clark was born in 1928 in Chicago and spent much of his life chasing her more notorious residents, including locating Sam Giancana several times, to the distress of the CIA.

After a reverse Rockwell childhood he escaped to Tucson, Arizona, where he euchred a precarious JD from the University of Arizona and won the heart of the lady by his side, 50 some summers now. They went directly into the FBI, living all over the country and the world. Mexico and London were magical. They retired to La Jolla, California, to write (J. Edgar is stirring uneasily) sketch (study and teach) and travel, (a dozen home exchanges in Europe). They have four lovely, lippy offspring scattered around the world carping about abuse and favoritism.

Printed in the United Kingdom
by Lightning Source UK Ltd.
102344UKS00001B/239